BUSINESS ECONOMICS IN A RAPIDLY-CHANGING WORLD

SMALL BUSINESS ADMINISTRATION HUBZONE PROGRAM: DISCUSSION AND DEBATE

BUSINESS ECONOMICS IN A RAPIDLY-CHANGING WORLD

Additional books in this series can be found on Nova's website under the Series tab.

Additional E-books in this series can be found on Nova's website under the E-book tab.

BUSINESS ISSUES, COMPETITION AND ENTREPRENEURSHIP

Additional books in this series can be found on Nova's website under the Series tab.

Additional E-books in this series can be found on Nova's website under the E-book tab.

BUSINESS ECONOMICS IN A RAPIDLY-CHANGING WORLD

SMALL BUSINESS ADMINISTRATION HUBZONE PROGRAM: DISCUSSION AND DEBATE

BRADLEY POWERS
AND
KYLE SIMONS
EDITOR

Nova Science Publishers, Inc.
New York

For permission to use material from this book please contact us:
Telephone 631-231-7269; Fax 631-231-8175
Web Site: http://www.novapublishers.com

Library of Congress Cataloging-in-Publication Data

Small Business Administration HUBZone program : discussion and debate / editors, Bradley Powers and Kyle Simons.
p. cm.
Includes index.
ISBN 978-1-62100-636-7 (softcover)
1. Small business--United States 2. Enterprise zones--United States. 3. Job creation--United States. 4. Public contracts--United States. 5. Community development, Urban--United States. 6. United States. Small Business Administration--Management--Evaluation. I. Powers, Bradley. II. Simons, Kyle.
HD2346.U5S594 2011
354.2'7990973--dc23

2011037426

Published by Nova Science Publishers, Inc. † New York

CONTENTS

PREFACE

The Small Business Administration (SBA) administers several programs to support small businesses, including the Historically Underutilized Business Zone Empowerment Contracting (HUBZone) program. The HUBZone program is a small business federal contracting assistance program "whose primary objective is job creation and increasing capital investment in distressed communities. It provides participating small businesses located in areas with low income, high poverty rates, or high unemployment rates with contracting opportunities in the form of "set-asides," sole-source awards, and price-evaluation preferences. This book examines the arguments presented both for and against targeting assistance to geographic areas within specified characteristics, as opposed to providing assistance to people or businesses with specified characteristics and discusses the HUBZone program's structure and operations.

Chapter 1- The Small Business Administration (SBA) administers several programs to support small businesses, including the Historically Underutilized Business Zone Empowerment Contracting (HUBZone) program. The HUBZone program is a small business federal contracting assistance program "whose primary objective is job creation and increasing capital investment in distressed communities." It provides participating small businesses located in areas with low income, high poverty rates, or high unemployment rates with contracting opportunities in the form of "set-asides," sole-source awards, and price-evaluation preferences.

Chapter 2- The HUBZone program remains vulnerable to fraud and abuse. Using falsified documents and employee information, GAO obtained HUBZone certification for three bogus firms using the addresses of the Alamo in Texas, a public storage facility in Florida, and a city hall in Texas as principal office locations. A simple Internet search by SBA could have revealed these as phony applications. While the agency has required more documentation in its application process since GAO's July 2008 report, GAO's testing shows that SBA does not adequately authenticate self-reported information and, for these cases, did not perform site visits to validate the addresses. Further, the changes have significantly increased the time it takes SBA to process applications. Specifically, SBA took 7 or more months to process each of the bogus applications—at least 6 months longer than for GAO's previous investigations. SBA continually lost documentation for GAO's fourth application, and eventually withdrew it after GAO failed to resubmit the same materials for the fourth time. On its Web site, SBA reported that applicants are experiencing delays during the application process.

Chapter 3- GAO found that fraud and abuse in the HUBZone program extends beyond the Washington, D.C., area. GAO identified 19 firms in Texas, Alabama, and California participating in the HUBZone program that clearly do not meet program requirements (i.e., principal office location or percentage of employees in HUBZone and subcontracting limitations). For example, one Alabama firm listed its principal office as "Suite 19," but when GAO investigators performed a site visit they found the office was in fact trailer 19 in a residential trailer park. The individual living in the trailer had no relationship to the HUBZone firm. In fiscal years 2006 and 2007, federal agencies obligated nearly $30 million to these 19 firms for performance as the prime contractor on HUBZone contracts and a total of $187 million on all federal contracts. The map below illustrates the geographical locations for the cases the authors examined.

In: Small Business Administration HUBZone ... ISBN: 978-1-62100-636-7
Editors: B. Powers and K. Simons

Chapter 1

SMALL BUSINESS ADMINISTRATION HUBZONE PROGRAM*

Robert Jay Dilger

SUMMARY

The Small Business Administration (SBA) administers several programs to support small businesses, including the Historically Underutilized Business Zone Empowerment Contracting (HUBZone) program. The HUBZone program is a small business federal contracting assistance program "whose primary objective is job creation and increasing capital investment in distressed communities." It provides participating small businesses located in areas with low income, high poverty rates, or high unemployment rates with contracting opportunities in the form of "set-asides," sole-source awards, and price-evaluation preferences.

In FY2010, the federal government awarded contracts valued at $12.7 billion to HUBZone certified businesses, with about $3.6 billion of that amount awarded through the HUBZone program. The program's FY2010 administrative cost was just under $17.0 million. Its FY2011 appropriation is $2.2 million, with the additional cost of administering the program provided by the SBA's appropriation for general administrative expenses.

---

* This is an edited, reformatted and augmented version of a Congressional Research Service publication, CRS Report for Congress R41268, from www.crs.gov, dated July 27, 2011.

Congressional interest in the HUBZone program has increased in recent years, primarily due to U.S. Government Accountability Office (GAO) reports of fraud in the program. Some Members have called for the program's termination. Others have recommended that the SBA continue its efforts to improve its administration of the program, especially its efforts to prevent fraud.

This report examines the arguments presented both for and against targeting assistance to geographic areas with specified characteristics, such as low income, high poverty, or high unemployment, as opposed to providing assistance to people or businesses with specified characteristics. It then assesses the arguments presented both for and against the creation and continuation of the HUBZone program, starting with the arguments presented during consideration of P.L. 105-135, the HUBZone Act of 1997 (Title VI of the Small Business Reauthorization Act of 1997), which authorized the program.

The report also discusses the HUBZone program's structure and operation, focusing on the definitions of HUBZone areas and HUBZone small businesses and the program's performance relative to federal contracting goals. The report includes an analysis of (1) the SBA's administration of the program, (2) the SBA's performance measures, and (3) the potential effect of the 2010 decennial census on which areas qualify as a HUBZone. The SBA has estimated that the eligibility of up to half of the currently certified HUBZone small businesses may be affected by the release of economic data from the 2010 decennial census.

This report also examines congressional action on P.L. 111-240, the Small Business Jobs Act of 2010, which amended the Small Business Act to remove certain language that had prompted federal courts and GAO to find that HUBZone set-asides have "precedence" over other small business set-asides. It also discusses H.R. 2131, the Protect HUBZones Act of 2011, and S. 633, the Small Business Contracting Fraud Prevention Act of 2011, which would extend for three years HUBZone eligibility for firms that lose their HUBZone eligibility due to the release of 2010 decennial census economic data. S. 633 would also require the SBA to implement several GAO recommendations designed to improve the SBA's administration of the program.

THE HUBZONE PROGRAM

The Small Business Administration (SBA) administers several programs to support small businesses, including the Historically Underutilized Business Zone Empowerment Contracting (HUBZone) program. The HUBZone program is "a place-based contracting assistance program whose primary objective is job creation and increasing capital investment in distressed communities."[1] It provides participating small businesses located in areas with low income, high poverty rates, or high unemployment rates with contracting opportunities in the form of "set-asides," sole-source awards, and price-evaluation preferences.[2]

The Competition in Contracting Act of 1984 generally requires "full and open competition" for government procurement contracts.[3] However, procurement set-asides are permissible competitive procedures. A set-aside restricts competition for a federal contract to specified contractors. Set-asides can be exclusive or partial, depending upon whether the entire procurement, or just part of it, is so restricted. In this case, the competition may be restricted to SBA-certified HUBZone businesses if there is a reasonable expectation of at least two SBA-certified HUBZone bidders and a fair market price. It is the most commonly used mechanism in the HUBZone program, accounting for about 86% of HUBZone program contracts and 70% of HUBZone program contract dollars. A sole-source award is a federal contract awarded, or proposed for award, without competition. Sole-source awards account for about 8% of HUBZone program contracts and 4% of HUBZone program contract dollars. Also, in any full and open competition for a federal contract "the price offered by a qualified HUBZone business shall be deemed as being lower than the price of another offeror if the HUBZone business price offer is not more than 10% higher than the other offer."[4] Price-evaluation preferences account for about 6% of HUBZone program contracts and 26% of HUBZone program contract dollars.[5]

In FY2010, the federal government awarded contracts valued at $12.7 billion to HUBZone certified businesses, with about $3.6 billion of that amount awarded through a HUBZone set-aside, sole source award, or price evaluation preference.[6] The program's FY2010 administrative cost was just under $17.0 million.[7] It received a FY2011 appropriation of $2.2 million, with the additional cost of administering the program covered by the SBA's appropriation for general administrative expenses.[8]

Congressional interest in the HUBZone program has increased in recent years, primarily due to U.S. Government Accountability Office (GAO) reports of fraud in the program. Some Members have called for the program's termination. Others have recommended that the SBA continue its efforts to improve its administration of the program, especially its efforts to prevent fraud.[9]

This report examines the arguments presented both for and against targeting assistance to geographic areas with specified characteristics, such as low income, high poverty, or high unemployment, as opposed to providing assistance to people or businesses with specified characteristics. It then assesses the arguments presented both for and against the creation and continuation of the HUBZone program, starting with the arguments presented during consideration of P.L. 105-135, the HUBZone Act of 1997 (Title VI of the Small Business Reauthorization Act of 1997), which authorized the program.

The report also discusses the HUBZone program's structure and operation, focusing on the definitions of HUBZone areas and HUBZone small businesses and the program's performance relative to federal contracting goals. The report includes an analysis of (1) the SBA's administration of the program, (2) the SBA's performance measures, and (3) the potential effect of the 2010 decennial census on which areas qualify as a HUBZone.

The SBA has estimated that "up to half of the currently certified HUBZone small business concerns may be affected by the results of the 2010 Decennial Census, whether as a result of the company's principal office losing HUBZone status or the company's employees no longer residing in a HUBZone."[10] About 27% of currently qualified census tracts, 47.5% of currently qualified non-metropolitan counties, and 30% of difficult development areas are expected to lose their HUBZone eligibility following the release of new economic data from the 2010 decennial census.[11]

This report also examines congressional action on P.L. 111-240, the Small Business Jobs Act of 2010, which amended the Small Business Act to remove certain language that had prompted federal courts and GAO to find that HUBZone set-asides have "precedence" over other small business set-asides. It also discusses H.R. 2131, the Protect HUBZones Act of 2011, and S. 633, the Small Business Contracting Fraud Prevention Act of 2011, which would extend for three years HUBZone eligibility for firms that lose their HUBZone eligibility due to the release of 2010 decennial census economic data. S. 633 would also require the SBA to implement several GAO recommendations designed to improve the SBA's administration of the program.

TARGETING ASSISTANCE TO GEOGRAPHIC AREAS

The HUBZone program was authorized by P.L. 105-135, the HUBZone Act of 1997 (Title VI of the Small Business Reauthorization Act of 1997).[12] Senator Christopher S. "Kit" Bond, the legislation's sponsor, described it as a "jobs bill and a welfare-to-work bill" designed to "create realistic opportunities for moving people off of welfare and into meaningful jobs" in "inner cities and rural counties that have low household incomes, high unemployment, and whose communities have suffered from a lack of investment."[13] Its enactment was part of a broader debate that had been underway since the late 1970s concerning whether the federal government should target assistance to geographic areas with specified characteristics, such as low income, high poverty, or high unemployment, as opposed to providing assistance to people or businesses with specified characteristics.

Discussion

The idea of targeting government assistance to geographic areas with specified characteristics, as opposed to targeting government assistance to people or businesses with specified characteristics, has its origins in a British experiment in urban revitalization started during the late 1970s. In 1978, Sir Geoffrey Howe, a Conservative member of Parliament, argued for the establishment of market-based enterprise zones, which provide government regulatory and tax relief, in economically distressed areas as a means to encourage entrepreneurs "to pursue profit with minimum governmental restrictions."[14] With the support of Prime Minister Margaret Thatcher's Conservative government (1979-1990), by the mid-1980s, more than two dozen enterprise zones were operating in England. Evaluations of the British enterprise zones' potential for having a positive effect on the long-term economic growth of economically distressed areas suggested that providing tax incentives and regulatory relief in those areas were "useful but not decisive economic development tools for distressed communities."[15]

In the United States, the idea of targeting regulatory and tax relief to economically distressed places appealed to some liberals who had become frustrated by the lack of progress some economically distressed communities had experienced under conventional government assistance programs, such as federal grant-in-aid programs. They tended to view the idea as a supplement to existing government assistance programs. Some conservatives also supported the idea of providing additional regulatory and tax relief to geographic areas because it generally aligned with their views on reducing government regulation and taxes. They tended to view it as a replacement, as opposed to a supplement, for existing government assistance programs.[16] As a result, support for targeting federal assistance to economically distressed places came from a diverse group of individuals and organizations that were often on opposing sides in other issue areas. Some of its leading proponents were the Congressional Black Caucus; the National Urban League; the National League of Cities; the National Association for the Advancement of Colored People; President Ronald Reagan; Republican Representative Jack Kemp, who introduced the first enterprise zone bill in Congress in May 1980 (H.R. 7240, the Urban Jobs and Enterprise Zone Act of 1980); and Democratic Representative Robert Garcia, who co-sponsored with Representative Kemp H.R. 3824, the Urban Jobs and Enterprise Zone Act of 1981.[17]

Opponents noted that targeting government assistance, in this case regulatory and tax relief, to economically distressed places would "provide incentives in designated areas, regardless of the nature of the industry which would benefit from the incentives."[18] They argued that it would be more efficient and cost effective to target federal assistance to businesses that offer primarily high-wage, full-time jobs with benefits and have relatively high multiplier effects on job creation than to offer the same benefits to all businesses, including those that offer primarily low-wage, part-time jobs with few or no benefits and have relatively low multiplier effects on job creation.[19]

Others opposed the idea because they viewed it as a partisan extension of supply-side economics.[20] Others, including the National Federation of Independent Businesses, an organization representing the interests of the nation's small businesses, were not convinced that providing "marginal rate reductions or marginal reductions in taxes" would "stimulate the entry of new businesses into depressed areas."[21] Also, some economists argued that it would be more efficient to let the private market determine where businesses locate rather than have the government enact policies that encourage businesses to locate, or relocate, in areas they would otherwise avoid. In their view, "the locational diversion of economic activity reduces or may outweigh gains from the creation of economic activity."[22]

These disagreements may have had a role in delaying the enactment of the first, fully functional federal enterprise zone program until 1993 (P.L. 103-66, the Omnibus Budget Reconciliation Act of 1993).[23] In the meantime, 37 states and the District of Columbia had initiated their own enterprise zone programs.[24] Evaluations of their effect on job creation and the economic status of the targeted distressed areas "provided conflicting conclusions, with some finding little or no program-related impacts, and others finding gains in the zones associated with the enterprise zone incentives."[25] Evaluations of federal enterprise zones would later reach similarly mixed findings.[26]

The Debate over HUBZones

The federal enterprise zone program's enactment in 1993 established a precedent for the enactment of other programs, such as the HUBZone program, that target federal assistance, in this case government contracts, to places with specified characteristics. For example, the Senate Committee on Small Business's report accompanying the HUBZone program's authorizing legislation in 1997 presented many of the same arguments for adopting the HUBZone program that had been presented for adopting the federal enterprise zone program:

> Creating new jobs in economically distressed areas has been the greatest challenge for many of our nation's governors, mayors, and community leaders. The trend is for business to locate in areas where there are customers and a skilled workforce. Asking a business to locate in a distressed area often seems counter to its potential to be successful. But without businesses in these communities, we don't create jobs, and without sources of new jobs, we are unlikely to have a successful revitalization effort.
>
> The HUBZone program attempts to utilize a valuable government resource, a government contract, and make it available to small businesses who agree in return to locate in an economically distressed area and employ people from these areas.... Contracts to small businesses in HUBZones can translate into thousands of job opportunities for persons who are unemployed or underemployed.[27]

HUBZone opponents expressed many of the same arguments that were raised in opposition to federal enterprise zones. For example, some Members opposed contract set-asides because they "unfairly discriminate against more efficient producers" and argued that "lower taxes, fewer mandates and freer markets are what stimulate the growth of small business."[28] Others argued that the experiences under enterprise zones suggested that HUBZones would have, at best, a limited impact on the targeted area's economic prospects:

> the record of enterprise zones demonstrates that businesses that locate in an area because of tax breaks or other artificial inducements (such as HUBZone contract preferences), instead of genuine competitive advantages, generally prove not to be sustainable.... Thus, the incentives generally go to businesses that would have located in and hired from the target area anyway.... Therefore, we should be realistic about the impact the HUBZone legislation will have on business relocation decisions.[29]

HUBZone critics also argued that it would compete with, and potentially diminish the effectiveness of, the SBA's Minority Small Business and Capital Ownership Development 8(a) program.[30] That program provides participating small businesses with training, technical assistance, and contracting opportunities in the form of set-asides and sole-source awards. Eligibility for the 8(a) program is generally limited to small businesses "unconditionally owned and controlled by one or more socially and economically disadvantaged individuals who are of good character and citizens of the United States" that demonstrate "potential for success."[31] Small businesses owned by Indian tribes, Alaska Native Corporations, Native Hawaiian Organizations, and Community Development Corporations are also eligible for the 8(a) program under somewhat different terms. In FY2008, 9,462 firms participated in the 8(a) program, and the federal government spent $6.3 billion on contracts with 8(a) firms.[32]

Others argued that the HUBZone self-certification process "while laudable in its effort to reduce certification costs and delays, invites inadvertent or deliberate abuses."[33]

As will be discussed in greater detail later, in recent years, the SBA's administration of the HUBZone program and the program's effectiveness in assisting economically distressed areas have been criticized. For example, the U.S. Government Accountability Office (GAO) has argued that the program is subject to fraud and abuse and has recommended that the SBA "take additional actions to certify and monitor HUBZone firms as well as to assess the results of the HUBZone program."[34] Also, several Members of Congress have questioned the program's effectiveness. For example, Representative Nydia M. Velázquez has argued that

> When first introduced, the HUBZone program promised to create opportunities for small businesses in low-income communities. It was designed to do this by helping entrepreneurs access the Federal marketplace. In theory, the benefits will be twofold; HUBZones will not only bolster the small business community, but will also breathe new life into struggling neighborhoods.
>
> However, the program has been undermined by chronic underfunding, inherent program flaws and sloppy management. Instead of being incubators for growth and development, HUBZones have become breeding grounds for fraud and abuse.[35]

HUBZone Areas Defined

There are currently five HUBZone types (or classes):

- qualified census tracts (QCTs),
- qualified non-metropolitan counties,
- qualified Indian Reservations/Indian Country,
- military bases closed under the Base Realignment and Closure Act (BRAC), and
- difficult development areas (DDAs).[36]

In addition, QCTs and qualified non-metropolitan counties that lose their eligibility due to the release of new economic data may temporarily retain their eligibility by becoming a redesignated area.

Qualified Census Tracts

QCTs are determined by the U.S. Housing and Urban Development (HUD) for its low-income housing tax credit program. The current criteria are

- at least 50% of households with income below 60% of the median gross income of the metropolitan statistical area (in metropolitan census tracts) or the median gross income for all non-metropolitan areas of the state (in non-metropolitan census tracts) or
- a poverty rate of at least 25%.[37]

About one-sixth (10,169) of all census tracts have QCT status.[38]

In the past, this economic data was only available from the decennial census. As a result, QCTs changed relatively infrequently, typically as new economic data from each decennial census became available or when the Census Bureau undertook a new delineation of census tracts. The Census Bureau reexamines its census tracts following each decennial census in an effort to keep them homogeneous with respect to population characteristics, economic status, and living conditions.[39] As a result of this delineation process, some census tracts may be enlarged and others may be split into two or more census tracts. This can cause a change in the census tract's QCT status. The typical census tract has between 1,500 and 8,000 persons.

Current QCT designations are based on census tract economic data from the 2000 decennial census. However, the Census Bureau no longer relies on the decennial census to collect this data at the census tract level. Instead, it relies on the American Community Survey (ACS). Although the ACS is an annual survey, census tract economic data from the ACS will be released as five-year averages. The first release of this economic data will cover the 2005 through 2009 period. The Census Bureau expects to make this data available in late 2010, or early 2011. HUD anticipates that it will review QCTs using the new economic data during 2011, with any changes effective as of January 1, 2012. QCTs will subsequently be reviewed based on the release of new ACS economic data every five years.[40]

Qualified Non-metropolitan Counties

A qualified non-metropolitan county is any county that "was not located in a metropolitan statistical area at the time of the most recent census taken for purposes of selecting qualified census tracts under section 42(d)(5)(C)(ii) of the Internal Revenue Code of 1986," and in which

- the median household income is less than 80% of the non-metropolitan state median household income, based on the most recent data available from the Bureau of the Census of the Department of Commerce or
- the unemployment rate is not less than 140% of the average unemployment rate for the United States or for the state in which such county is located, whichever is less, based on the most recent data available from the Secretary of Labor.[41]

About 24% (719) of all counties have qualified non-metropolitan county status.[42]

In the past, the non-metropolitan county's median household income was derived from decennial census data. If a county qualified on this basis, its HUBZone status was "secure until publication of the data from the following census."[43] However, the Census Bureau now relies on the ACS to collect that data. The Census Bureau expects to release the economic data needed to determine the eligibility of non-metropolitan counties based on median household income in late 2010. As a result, the SBA will "generate a new list of qualified non-metropolitan counties at that time that will take into consideration the analysis of income data coming from the five year ACS."[44] The eligibility of qualified non-metropolitan counties based on median household income will subsequently be reviewed based on the release of new ACS economic data every five years.[45]

The non-metropolitan county's unemployment rate is derived from data released annually by the Department of Labor's Bureau of Labor Statistics. As a result, if a county qualifies, or fails to qualify, on this basis, its HUBZone status can change as new unemployment data is released. As will be discussed, Congress created redesignated areas to delay the loss of HUBZone status for areas that lose HUBZone eligibility due to the release of new economic data.

The qualified non-metropolitan county designation is the only type of HUBZone that is determined by the SBA. The formula is set in law and the data is derived from other agencies, but the designation is made by the SBA.[46]

Qualified Indian Reservation/Indian Country

P.L. 105-135, the HUBZone Act of 1997 (Title VI of the Small Business Reauthorization Act of 1997), provided HUBZone eligibility to "lands within the external boundaries of an Indian reservation." Since then, the term "Indian reservation" has been clarified and expanded to include

- Indian trust lands and other lands covered under the term "Indian Country" as used by the Bureau of Indian Affairs,
- portions of the state of Oklahoma designated as former Indian reservations by the Internal Revenue Service (Oklahoma tribal statistical areas), and
- Alaska Native village statistical areas.[47]

There are 659 qualified Indian reservations, Oklahoma tribal statistical areas, and Alaska Native village statistical areas.[48] A private firm's analysis of Indian reservation's economic characteristics conducted on behalf of the SBA indicated that

> for the most part—and particularly in states where reservations are numerous and extensive—mean income of reservations is far below state levels, and unemployment rates and poverty rates are far above

state levels. There are some interesting exceptions, however, where reservations are basically on a par with the states they are in. Examples include Osage reservation in Oklahoma and reservations in Connecticut, Rhode Island, and Michigan. The factors at work here may be casinos and oil.[49]

Military Bases Closed under BRAC

P.L. 108-447, the Consolidated Appropriations Act, 2005, provided HUBZone eligibility for five years to "lands within the external boundaries of a military installation closed through a privatization process" under the authority of P.L. 101-510, the Defense Base Closure and Realignment Act of 1990 (BRAC—Title XXIX of the National Defense Authorization Act for Fiscal Year 1991). The military base's HUBZone eligibility commences on the effective date of the law (December 8, 2004) if the military base was already closed at that time, or on the date of formal closure if the military base was still operational at that time.

Forty-eight military bases closed under BRAC are currently designated as a HUBZone.[50]

Difficult Development Areas

P.L. 109-59, the Safe, Accountable, Flexible, Efficient Transportation Equity Act: A Legacy for Users (SAFETEA), provided HUBZone eligibility to difficult development areas (DDAs) within "Alaska, Hawaii, or any territory or possession of the United States outside the 48 contiguous states."[51] These areas are designated annually by the Secretary of HUD "in accordance with section 42(d)(5)(C)(iii) of the Internal Revenue Code" which applies to HUD's low-income housing tax credit program.[52] This section of the Internal Revenue Code defines a DDA "as areas designated by the Secretary of Housing and Urban Development as having high construction, land, and utility costs relative to area median gross income."[53] These areas may not exceed 20% of the population of a metropolitan statistical area or of a non-metropolitan area.

There are 47 HUBZone DDAs.[54]

Redesignated Areas

One of the implicit goals of the HUBZone program is to improve the economic standing of the geographic areas receiving assistance so that they are no longer an economically distressed area. As a result, it could be argued that it is a program success when a QCT or a qualified non-metropolitan county loses its qualification as a HUBZone area when new economic data are published. However, because "small business concerns that locate to a HUBZone may lose their eligibility in only one year due to changes in such data" and out of concern that some HUBZone areas could "shift in and out of eligibility year after year," Congress included a provision in P.L. 106-554, the HUBZones in Native America Act of 2000 (Title VI, the Consolidated Appropriations Act, 2001), to address this issue.[55] The provision provided census tracts and non-metropolitan counties that lose HUBZone eligibility due to the release of new economic data an automatic extension "for the 3-year period following the date on which the census tract or nonmetropolitan county ceased to be so qualified."[56] The act labeled census tracts and non-metropolitan counties that receive an extension of HUBZone eligibility "redesignated areas."

Subsequently, P.L. 108-447, the Consolidated Appropriations Act, 2005, effectively extended the eligibility of HUBZone redesignated areas by allowing them to retain eligibility for three years or until the public release of data from the 2010 Census, whichever is later:

> Redesignated area means any census tract or any non-metropolitan county that ceases to be a qualified HUBZone, except that such census tracts or nonmetropolitan counties may be "redesignated areas" only until the later of: (1) The date on which the Census Bureau publicly releases the first results from the 2010 decennial census; or (2) Three years after the date on which the census tract or non-metropolitan county ceased to be so qualified.
>
> The date on which the census tract or non-metropolitan county ceases to be qualified is the date that the official government data, which affects the eligibility of the HUBZone, is released to the public.[57]

In 2008, GAO compared the economic characteristics of QCTs and qualified non-metropolitan counties to redesignated areas. It reported that it "found a marked difference" in their economic characteristics. For example, GAO reported that approximately 60% of QCTs (excluding redesignated areas) had a poverty rate of 30% or more compared to approximately 4% of redesignated QCTs. Also, about 75% of QCTs (excluding redesignated areas) had a median household income that was less than 60% of the metropolitan area median household income compared to about 10% of redesignated QCTs.[58]

There are 3,760 redesignated HUBZone census tracts, 651 redesignated HUBZone non-metropolitan counties, and 20 redesignated HUBZone DDAs.[59] The SBA has indicated that all redesignated HUBZones due to expire on "the date on which the Census Bureau publicly releases the first results from the 2010 Decennial Census" will expire on October 1, 2011.[60] The redesignated HUBZones that will lose their eligibility are the ones that were provided an extended grandfathering period beyond the original three years, until the Census Bureau released new data collected from the 2010 census.[61]

HUBZone Businesses Defined

Firms must be certified by the SBA to participate in the HUBZone program. There are currently 8,533 certified HUBZone businesses.[62] To become certified, firms complete and submit specified SBA HUBZone application forms to the SBA, either online or by mail. Firms must

- meet SBA size standards for the firm's primary industry classification;
- be at least 51% owned and controlled by U.S. citizens, or a Community Development Corporation, an agricultural cooperative, or an Indian tribe (including Alaska Native Corporations and Native Hawaiian Organizations);
- maintain a principal office located in a HUBZone;
- ensure that at least 35% of its employees reside in a HUBZone;[63]
- represent, as provided in the application, that it will "attempt to maintain" having 35% of its employees reside in a HUBZone during the performance of any HUBZone contract it receives;
- represent, as provided in the application, that it will ensure that it will comply with certain contract performance requirements in connection

with contracts awarded to it as a qualified HUBZone small business concern (such as spending at least 50% of the cost of the contract incurred for personnel on its own employees or employees of other qualified HUBZone small business concerns and meeting specified subcontracting limitations to nonqualified HUBZone small business concerns);

- provide an active up-to-date Dun and Bradstreet profile and Data Universal Numbering System (DUNS) number that represents the business; and
- provide an active Central Contractor Registration profile for the business.[64]

Until recently, the SBA's goal was to make its determination within 30 calendar days after receipt of a complete application package, subject to the need for additional information or clarification of information contained in the application. As will be discussed, in response to reports of applicant fraud, the SBA has reengineered its applicant review process and now takes, depending on the complexity of the application and the need for additional information, from 5 to 12 months to make its determination.

If the SBA approves the application, it will send a written notice to the business and automatically enter it on a list of certified HUBZone businesses. A decision to deny eligibility must be in writing, and state the specific reasons for denial.[65]

In the past, the SBA's staff conducted random program examinations "to verify the accuracy of any certification made or information provided as part of the HUBZone application process, or in connection with a HUBZone contract."[66] Examiners typically verified that the business met the program's eligibility requirements, and that it met such requirements at the time of its application for certification, its most recent recertification, or its certification in connection with a HUBZone contract.[67] In response to reports of fraud, the SBA, in addition to reengineering its applicant review process, now conducts program examinations of all firms that received a HUBZone contract in the previous fiscal year.[68]

Certified HUBZone small business concerns must recertify every three years to the SBA that they meet the requirements for being a HUBZone business.[69] They must also immediately notify the SBA of any material change that could affect their eligibility, such as a change in the ownership, business structure, or principal office of the concern, or a failure to meet the 35% HUBZone residency requirement.[70]

HUBZone Federal Contracting Goals

Since 1978, federal agency heads have been required "to establish goals for small business participation in specified federal procurement contracts and to consult with and report to the SBA about such goals and their realization."[71] In 1988, Congress authorized the President to annually establish government-wide minimum participation goals for procurement contracts awarded to small businesses and small businesses owned and controlled by socially and economically disadvantaged individuals. Congress required the government-wide minimum participation goal for small businesses to be "not less than 20% of the total value of all prime contract awards for each fiscal year" and "not less than 5% of the total value of all prime contract and subcontract awards for each fiscal year" for small businesses owned and controlled by socially and economically disadvantaged individuals.[72] Each federal agency was directed to "have an annual goal that presents, for that agency, the maximum practicable opportunity for small business concerns and small business concerns owned and controlled by socially and economically disadvantaged individuals to participate in the performance of contracts let by such agency."[73] The SBA was also required to report to the President annually on the attainment of the goals and to include the information in an annual report to the Congress.[74]

The SBA negotiates contracting goals with each federal agency and evaluates the agencies' performance against these goals annually, using data from the Federal Procurement Data System—Next Generation, managed by the U.S. General Services Administration. This information is compiled into the official Small Business Goaling Report, which the SBA releases annually.

There are no punitive consequences for not meeting the small business procurement goals. However, the SBA's Small Business Goaling Report is distributed widely, receives media attention, and serves to heighten public awareness of the issue of small business contracting. For example, agency performance as reported in the SBA's Small Business Goaling Report is often cited by Members during their questioning of federal agency witnesses during congressional hearings.

P.L. 105-135, the HUBZone Act of 1997 (Title VI of the Small Business Reauthorization Act of 1997), increased the federal government-wide goal for contracting with small businesses from 20% to 23%. It also established the following contracting goals for the HUBZone program: not less than 1% of the total value of all prime contract awards for FY1999, not less than 1.5% for FY2000, not less than 2% for FY2001, not less than 2.5% for FY2002, and not less than 3% for FY2003 and each fiscal year thereafter. P.L. 111-240, the

Small Business Jobs Act of 2010, amended the HUBZone contracting goal to include the total value of all prime contract awards and subcontract awards.[75]

The current federal small business contracting goals are

- at least 23% of the total value of all prime contact awards to small businesses for each fiscal year,
- 5% of the total value of all prime contact awards and subcontract awards to small disadvantaged businesses for each fiscal year,
- 5% of the total value of all prime contact awards and subcontract awards to women-owned small businesses,
- 3% of the total value of all prime contact awards and subcontract awards to HUBZone small businesses, and
- 3% of the total value of all prime contact awards and subcontract awards to service-disabled veteran-owned small businesses.[76]

Table 1. Federal Contracting Goals and Percent of FY2010 Federal Contract Dollars Awarded to Small Businesses, by Type

Business Type	Federal Goal	Percentage of FY2010 Federal Contract Dollars
Small Businesses	23.0%	20.3%
Small Disadvantaged Businesses	5.0%	7.0%
Women-Owned Small Businesses	5.0%	4.4%
HUBZone Small Businesses	3.0%	2.4%
Service-Disabled Veteran-	3.0%	2.2%
Owned Small Businesses		

Source: U.S. Small Business Administration, "Government-Wide Performance: 2009 Small Business Procurement Scorecard," Washington, DC, http://www.sba.gov/sites/default/files/files/govt_wide_2009.pdf (federal goals); and U.S. General Services Administration, Federal Procurement Data System - Next Generation, Washington, DC, https://www.fpds.gov/fpdsng/ (contract dollars).

Notes: The total amount awarded in FY2010 was $537.8 billion, with $108.8 billion to small businesses, $37.7 billion to small disadvantaged businesses, $23.5 billion to women owned small businesses, $12.7 billion to SBA-certified HUBZone small businesses, and $12.1 billion to service-disabled veteran-owned small businesses.

As shown in Table 1, in FY2010, federal agencies met the federal contracting goal for small disadvantaged businesses, but not the other goals. Federal agencies awarded 20.3% of the value of their contracts to small businesses, 7.0% to small disadvantaged businesses, 4.4% to women-owned small businesses, 2.4% to HUBZone small businesses, and 2.2% to service-disabled veteran-owned small businesses.[77]

CONGRESSIONAL ISSUES

As mentioned previously, congressional interest in the HUBZone program has increased in recent years, primarily due to reports of fraud in the program. GAO was asked by Congress to review the SBA's administration of the HUBZone program and it has issued several recommendations designed to strengthen the SBA's fraud control measures.[78] GAO has also argued that the SBA lacks adequate performance measures to determine the HUBZone program's effect on the economically distressed areas it is designed to assist.[79]

Another issue of congressional interest is the potential effect of the release of 2010 decennial census data on HUBZone area eligibility. About one-third of QCTs (3,364 of 9,964) lost their HUBZone eligibility following the release of the 2000 decennial census data and almost as many census tracts (3,313) gained HUBZone eligibility.[80]

As will be discussed, Congress is currently considering legislation that would require the SBA to implement GAO's recommendations concerning the SBA's administration of the program and to revise the SBA's HUBZone performance measures. Congress is also considering legislation that would extend HUBZone eligibility for those HUBZone areas that lose eligibility due to the release of 2010 decennial census data.

In addition, Congress recently addressed the potential consequence of two Court of Federal Claims decisions that directed federal agencies to provide HUBZone set-asides preference when two or more set-aside programs could potentially be used.[81] Providing the HUBZone program preference over other small business contracting programs could have resulted in an increase in the percentage of federal contract dollars awarded to HUBZone small businesses and a decrease in the percentage of federal contract dollars awarded to other small businesses. P.L. 111-240, the Small Business Jobs Act of 2010, amended the Small Business Act (15 U.S.C. 657a(b)(2)(B)) to remove the language that the court relied upon in finding that HUBZone set-asides have "precedence." Specifically, P.L. 111-240 struck "a contract opportunity shall" and replaced it with "a contract opportunity may."[82] The court had ruled that the use of the word shall made the HUBZone program mandatory, whereas the use of the word may in the Section 8(a) contracting program for small businesses owned and controlled by the socially and economically disadvantaged made it a discretionary program, and mandatory programs took precedence over discretionary ones.[83]

Also, on October 1, 2010, the maximum contract award amounts that federal officials can set-aside for sole source awards under various small business contracting programs were increased to adjust for inflation.[84] For example, the maximum sole source contract award amounts for the HUBZone program were increased from not exceeding $5.5 million for manufacturing contracts or $3.5 million for other contract opportunities to not exceeding $6.5 million for manufacturing contracts or $4.0 million for other contract opportunities. It could be argued that these changes will make it difficult to compare the results of the federal government's small business procurement goaling program with previous year results and diminishes the goaling program's value as a tool to measure federal agency progress in awarding contracts to small businesses. It is possible that Congress may consider proposals to adjust the goals to account for these changes.

Program Administration

SBA's Office of Inspector General Audits

The SBA's administration of the HUBZone program has been criticized for a number of years. In 2003, the SBA's Office of Inspector General (OIG) completed an audit of 15 HUBZone firms operating in Idaho Falls, ID, after receiving a complaint that a relatively large number of certified HUBZone firms in that city may not be qualified to participate in the program.[85] At that time, HUBZone businesses self-certified in their application materials that they met the requirements for being a HUBZone business. Validating documentation, such as a copy of a business owner's birth certificate as proof of U.S. citizenship or a copy of the lease agreement to verify the business concern's principal office's location within a qualified HUBZone, were not required. The SBA OIG's audit found that

> over two-thirds of the 15 subject companies were either not in compliance with HUBZone eligibility requirements or had presumably gone out of business. We also found that the Office of HUBZone Empowerment's internal controls were inadequate to ensure that only eligible firms are certified and remain certified. Therefore, there is little assurance that the program will provide increased employment, investment and economic development for depressed areas. Since

ineligible companies could receive HUBZone contracts, the program is also vulnerable to federal contacting fraud.[86]

As a result of that audit, the SBA revised its program examination and recertification processes to provide "a more careful review" of HUBZone applications and implemented an online application process that was designed to "prescreen" potential applicants, "resulting in only those most-qualified actually submitting a completed application."[87] Citing the efficiencies brought about by the automation of HUBZone applications, the SBA reduced the number of staff in the Office of the HUBZone Program, which was responsible for program examinations, from 12 full-time equivalent employees in 2004 to eight in 2006.[88]

In 2006, the SBA OIG reported that there was a two-year backlog in HUBZone program examinations. It reported that it was concerned "that workload resources had not been adequately devoted to eliminating this two-year backlog" and firms that should be decertified from the program remained on the list of certified HUBZone businesses and potentially were "inappropriately receiving HUBZone contracts between the time they are initially certified and subsequently examined/recertified."[89]

As a result of the SBA OIG's second, follow-up audit of the HUBZone program, the SBA committed to reviewing 5% of all certifications "through a full-scale program of examinations."[90] The audit also resulted in heightened congressional attention to the issue of potential fraud within the HUBZone program.

GAO's Audits

In 2007, Representative Nydia M. Velázquez, then-chair of the House Committee on Small Business, asked GAO to review the HUBZone program, including the criteria and processes that the SBA uses to identify and map HUBZone areas, the mechanisms the SBA uses to ensure that only eligible small businesses participate in the program, and the actions the SBA has taken to assess the program's results.[91]

GAO conducted its audit of the SBA's administration of the HUBZone program from August 2007 through June 2008. It reported on June 17, 2008, that

- the map used by the SBA to publicize qualified HUBZone areas was inaccurate, resulting in ineligible small businesses participating in the program and excluding eligible businesses;

- the mechanisms used by the SBA to certify and monitor HUBZone firms provided limited assurance that only eligible firms participated in the program;
- the SBA had not complied with its own policy of recertifying HUBZone firms every three years (about 40% of those firms had not been recertified); and
- the SBA lacked formal guidance that would specify a time frame for processing HUBZone firm decertifications (1,400 of 3,600 firms proposed for decertification had not been processed within the SBA's self-imposed goal of 60 days).[92]

GAO released another report on the HUBZone program on July 17, 2008. It reported that it had "identified substantial vulnerabilities in SBA's application and monitoring process, clearly demonstrating that the HUBZone program is vulnerable to fraud and abuse."[93] Using fictitious employee information and fabricated documentation, GAO obtained HUBZone certification for four bogus firms. In one of its applications, GAO claimed that its principal office was the same address as a coffee store that happened to be located in a HUBZone. GAO argued that if the SBA "had performed a simple Internet search on the address, it would have been alerted to this fact."[94] Two of GAO's applications used leased mailboxes from retail postal services centers. GAO argued that "a post office box clearly does not meet SBA's principal office requirement."[95] In addition, it identified "10 firms from the Washington, D.C. metro area that were participating in the HUBZone program even though they clearly did not meet eligibility requirements."[96]

The SBA responded to GAO's findings by announcing that it would undertake "a complete re-engineering of the program" designed to

- ensure that its HUBZone maps were up-to-date, and
- minimize program risk by collecting additional supporting documentation of all HUBZone applicants to support program eligibility.[97]

In response to GAO's findings and the SBA's response to those findings, Representative Velázquez asked GAO to determine "whether cases of fraud and abuse in the HUBZone program exist outside of the Washington, D.C. metropolitan area" and to assess the SBA's efforts to establish an effective fraud prevention system for the HUBZone program.[98]

On March 25, 2009, GAO reported that, as of that date

- the SBA had updated its HUBZone map but had not implemented procedures to ensure that it remains accurate,
- had made little progress in ensuring the eligibility of firms in the HUBZone program, and
- had eliminated its backlog of recertifications but had not established a process or procedures to prevent future backlogs.[99]

GAO also reported that it had selected four geographical areas for analysis to determine whether cases of fraud and abuse exist for HUBZone businesses located outside of the Washington, DC, metropolitan area: Dallas, TX; Huntsville, AL; San Antonio, TX; and San Diego, CA. GAO conducted its analysis of HUBZone businesses in those four areas from September 2008 through March 2009. GAO reported that it found "fraud and abuse" in all four metropolitan areas, including 19 firms that "clearly are not eligible" and highlighted 10 firms that it "found to be egregiously out of compliance with HUBZone program requirements."[100]

The SBA responded to GAO's audits and congressional criticism of its administration of the HUBZone program by "reengineering business processes to reduce fraud and abuse within the program."[101] In 2009, it "moved from verifying a sample of HUBZone firms to verifications of 100% of HUBZone firms receiving contracts in the previous fiscal year."[102] In 2010, the SBA reported that its standard HUBZone business process

> now requires all firms to submit supporting documentation verifying the information and statements made in their application. Previous practice required firms only to submit an electronic application.
>
> In addition, the Program Office implemented a new business process for recertifying HUBZone firms which requires all firms that are due for recertification to certify via wet signature that they still conform to the eligibility requirements. Previous practice required firms to submit an electronic verification.[103]

Karen Mills, the SBA's Administrator, testified before the House Committee on Small Business on April 21, 2010, that the SBA is "working to ensure that only legitimate and eligible firms are benefiting from HUBZone" and has "made dramatic increases in the number of site visits to HUBZone firms—from less than 100 in 2008 to over 900 in 2009. We're on track to do more than 1,000 this year."[104]

The SBA's new, more labor intensive certification process, coupled with an increase in applications for HUBZone certifications, resulted in what the

SBA described as "significant delays in the processing of new applications for certification."[105] Noting that individual applications "can very greatly depending on the complexity of the case and the applicant's responsiveness to any requests for supporting information," the SBA reported that the final HUBZone determination time frames currently "vary from 5 months to 12 months, with an average of 8 to 10 months."[106]

Recognizing that its processing time to certify HUBZone businesses may have adverse consequences for at least some of these businesses, the SBA placed on its website an explanation for the processing delays and the following notice to HUBZone applicants:

> The SBA processing delays are a serious issue for applicants, especially for those wishing to bid on upcoming HUBZone contracts. Therefore, if you are a firm which has a pending application in process for more than 4 months and has an upcoming HUBZone set-aside contract on which it would like to bid, please contact our Help Desk to determine if we can provide you with a decision quickly.[107]

On June 25, 2010, GAO released another report concerning the SBA's efforts to reduce fraud in the HUBZone program. GAO submitted applications for HUBZone certification for "four new bogus firms ... using false information and fabricated documents ... fictitious employee information and bogus principal office addresses" including "the addresses of the Alamo in Texas, a public storage facility in Florida, and a city hall in Texas as principal office locations."[108] The SBA certified three of the four bogus firms and lost GAO's documentation for its fourth application "on multiple occasions," forcing GAO to abandon that application.[109] GAO reported that "the SBA continues to struggle with reducing fraud risks in its HUBZone certification process despite reportedly taking steps to bolster its controls."[110] It reported that

> A simple Internet search by SBA could have revealed these as phony applications. While the agency has required more documentation in its application process since GAO's July 2008 report, GAO's testing shows that SBA does not adequately authenticate self-reported information and, for these cases, did not perform site visits to validate the addresses. Further, the changes have significantly increased the time it takes SBA to process applications. Specifically, SBA took 7 or more months to process each of the bogus applications—at least 6 months longer than for GAO's previous investigations.[111]

GAO also reported that in response to their test, SBA officials "stated that it was unreasonable to expect them to have identified our fictitious firms because of bogus documentation that we included in our applications," that "the submission of false affidavits would subject an applicant to prosecution," and that "competitors may identify fraudulent firms and likely protest if those firms were awarded a HUBZone contract."[112] GAO also reported that SBA officials stated that "because of resource constraints, they primarily conduct site visits on certified firms that receive large prime HUBZone contracts."[113] GAO argued that "while the threat of prosecution is an important deterrent, it does not help to identify firms that attempt to commit fraud, as our testing shows."[114] GAO also argued that "while competitors may identify some ineligible firms that were awarded contracts, SBA is responsible for ensuring that only eligible firms participate in the HUBZone program."[115] GAO also reported that "if the SBA had conducted site visits at the addresses of the firms represented in our applications, those applications would have been identified as fraudulent."[116]

Legislation

H.R. 2131, the Protect HUBZones Act of 2011, was introduced on June 3, 2011, and was referred to the House Committee on Small Business. It would extend the redesignated status of HUBZone areas that lose that status due to the release of economic data from the 2010 decennial census for three years after the first date on which the SBA publishes a HUBZone map that is based on the results from the 2010 decennial census.

S. 633, the Small Business Contracting Fraud Prevention Act of 2011, was introduced on March 17, 2011, and has been referred to the Senate Committee on Small Business and Entrepreneurship. It would require the SBA to implement GAO's recommendations to

- maintain a correct, accurate, and updated map to identify HUBZone areas,
- implement policies that ensure only eligible firms participate in the program,
- employ appropriate technology to control costs and maximize efficiency,
- notify the Small Business Committees of any backlogs in applications or recertifications with plans and timetables for eliminating the back log,

- ensure small businesses meet the 35% HUBZone residency requirement at the time of bid as well as contract award, and
- extend the redesignated status of HUBZone areas that lose that status due to the release of economic data from the 2010 decennial census for three years after the first date on which the SBA publishes a HUBZone map that is based on the results from the 2010 decennial census.[117]

The SBA has not formally responded to the legislation. It has argued at congressional hearings and in its FY2012 congressional budget justification report that it is taking steps to implement GAO's recommendations.[118]

Performance Measures

As part of its 2008 audit of the HUBZone program, GAO reported that the SBA had taken "limited steps" to assess the effectiveness of the HUBZone program.[119] It noted that the SBA's performance measures—the number of applications approved and recertifications processed, the annual value of federal contracts awarded to HUBZone firms, and the number of program examinations completed—provide data on program activity but "do not directly measure the program's effect on firms (such as growth in employment or changes in capital investment) or directly measure the program's effect on the communities in which the firms are located (for instance, changes in median household income or poverty levels)."[120] GAO recommended that the SBA "further develop measures and implement plans to assess the effectiveness of the HUBZone program that take into account factors such as the economic characteristics of the HUBZone area."[121]

The SBA responded to GAO's findings by announcing that it "would develop an assessment tool to measure the economic benefits that accrue to areas in the HUBZone program" and that they "would then issue periodic reports accompanied by the underlying data."[122]

On March 25, 2009, GAO reported that, as of that date, the SBA had not developed measures or implemented plans to assess the program's effectiveness.[123] GAO noted that the SBA did commission an independent review of the HUBZone program's economic impact. That study was released in May 2008. It concluded that the HUBZone program

> has not generated enough HUBZone contract dollars to have an impact on a national scale. When spread over an eight-year period across 2,450 metropolitan areas and counties with qualified census tracts, qualified counties, and Indian reservations, \$6 billion has a limited impact....
>
> About two-thirds of HUBZone areas have HUBZone businesses; just under one-third have HUBZone vendors that have won HUBZone contracts; and about 4 percent of HUBZone areas have received annual-equivalent HUBZone contract revenues greater than \$100 per capita, based on HUBZone population....
>
> The program has a substantial impact in only a very small percentage of HUBZones. Where the impact is largest, there generally is at least one very successful vender in the HUBZone. Thus, the program can be effective. At present, however, the impact in two-thirds of all HUBZones is nil.[124]

GAO also noted that the SBA had issued a notice in the *Federal Register* on August 11, 2008, seeking public comment on a proposed methodology for measuring the economic impact of the HUBZone program.[125] The notice presented a two-step economic model that the SBA had developed to estimate the impact directly attributable to the HUBZone program, the SBA's non-HUBZone programs, and other related federal procurement programs on HUBZone areas. The notice indicated that economic impact "will be measured by the estimated growth in median household income and employment (or a reduction in unemployment) in a specific HUBZone area."[126]

GAO criticized the SBA for relying on public comments to refine the proposed methodology "rather than conducting a comprehensive effort" that considered relevant literature and input from experts in economics and performance measurement.[127] GAO concluded that "based on our review, we do not believe this effort was a sound process for developing measures to assess the effectiveness of the program" and reported that the SBA had abandoned that proposal and "had initiated a new effort to address this issue."[128]

The SBA indicated in its FY2011 budget justification report to Congress that it had developed "a methodology for measuring the economic impact of the HUBZone program" in order to "provide for the continuous study and monitoring of the program's effectiveness in terms of its economic goals."[129] However, it did not provide any details concerning the methodology and has continued to use its previous performance measures—the number of small businesses assisted (applications approved and recertifications processed), the annual value of federal contracts awarded to HUBZone firms, and the number of program examinations completed—to assess the program's performance.[130]

Legislation

S. 633, the Small Business Contracting Fraud Prevention Act of 2011, would require the SBA to implement GAO's recommendation to "develop measures and implement plans to assess the effectiveness of the HUBZone program."[131] It would also require the SBA to identify "a baseline point in time to allow the assessment of economic development under the HUBZone program, including creating additional jobs" and take into account "the economic characteristics of the HUBZone and contracts being counted under multiple socioeconomic subcategories."[132]

The SBA has not formally responded to the legislation. It has argued at congressional hearings and in its FY2012 congressional budget justification report that it is taking steps to implement GAO's recommendation.[133]

One possible option available to Congress to further evaluate the HUBZone program's impact on small businesses and economically distressed communities is to require the SBA to commission a multi-year time series study of the HUBZone program's impact on small businesses and economically distressed communities similar to the multi-year time series study currently underway for the SBA's education and training programs.[134] That ongoing study, started in 2003, includes an annual survey of small business owners who have received SBA education and training services. The study's latest report, released on September 13, 2010, "measures attitudinal assessments, perceptions of changes in management/marketing practices, and business growth for firms that utilized the SBA's Entrepreneurial Development Resources [Small Business Development Centers, SCORE, and Women Business Centers] during the late summer or early fall of 2007, 2008 or 2009."[135]

The 2010 Decennial Census

As mentioned previously, P.L. 108-447, the Consolidated Appropriations Act, 2005, effectively extended the eligibility of redesignated HUBZone areas by allowing them to retain eligibility for three years or until the public release of data from the 2010 decennial census, whichever is later. At that time, based on past practice, it was anticipated that the Census Bureau would take at least a year, and probably longer, to release the economic data contained in the

2010 decennial census that would be used in the determination of HUBZone area status.[136] In the past, such data were derived from the decennial census long form. However, the census long form has been replaced by the American Community Survey (ACS), an ongoing mailed survey of about 250,000 households per month that gathers largely the same data as the long-form. The ACS collects and produces population and housing information at one-year, three-year, and five-year intervals, instead of every 10 years.[137] Specifically, the ACS

> provides annual data for areas with populations of at least 65,000 persons, including the total United States, all states and the District of Columbia, all congressional districts, about 800 counties, and 500 metropolitan and micropolitan statistical areas. For less populous areas, the Bureau is producing multi-year averages based on ACS data collected over several years. In 2008, the Bureau released the first three-year averages for areas with 20,000 or more persons, and by 2010, five-year averages will be available for areas with fewer than 20,000 persons.[138]

Because this is the first time that ACS data will be used in the determination of HUBZone area status it is possible that questions might be raised concerning the reliability of the survey data. However, the census long form was also a survey, with a 17% sample size in 2000.

It is also possible that questions might be raised concerning the impact of having economic data that was formerly available once every 10 years now being available once every five years. The SBA has indicated that QCTs and qualified nonmetropolitan counties will be reviewed based on ACS economic data every five years instead of waiting for the release of the next decennial census data.[139] It could be argued that using ACS data every five years may increase the HUBZone program's effectiveness in targeting assistance to areas most in need. The counter-argument is that increasing the frequency of QCT and qualified nonmetropolitan county determinations could limit the ability of at least some certified HUBZone businesses to benefit from the program.

Legislation

H.R. 2131, the Protect HUBZones Act of 2011, and S. 633, the Small Business Contracting Fraud Prevention Act of 2011, would effectively prolong the eligibility of at least some redesignated HUBZones. These bills would amend the Small Business Act to allow redesignated HUBZone areas to retain their HUBZone eligibility for three years or until three years after the first date on which the SBA publishes a HUBZone map that is based on the results from the 2010 decennial census, whichever is later. Current law allows HUBZone redesignated areas to retain eligibility for three years or until the public release of data from the 2010 decennial census, whichever is later. As mentioned previously, about one-third of QCTs in 2000 (3,364 of 9,964) lost their HUBZone eligibility following the release of the 2000 decennial census data and almost as many census tracts (3,313) gained HUBZone eligibility.[140]

CONCLUDING OBSERVATIONS

Congressional interest in the SBA's HUBZone program has increased in recent years to levels not seen since the initial debate over whether the program should be authorized. Debates over the program's effect on economically distressed communities, as reflected in GAO's recommendation for new SBA performance measures; concerns, which were addressed by P.L. 111-240, the Small Business Jobs Act of 2010, over the potential impact of the U.S. Court of Federal Claims ruling in *Mission Critical Solutions v. United States* providing the HUBZone program preference in federal contracting when two or more federal contract set-aside programs could be used; and the potential impact of the 2010 decennial census on which areas qualify as a HUBZone have all served to elevate congressional interest in the program. But perhaps the most influential reason for the increased level of congressional interest has been GAO's finding of fraud in the program.

The SBA has attempted to overhaul the program. It reported in its FY2011 congressional budget justification that it had "met its primary goal during FY2009" to reengineer its "business processes to reduce fraud and abuse with the program."[141] On April 21, 2010, SBA Administrator Karen Mills testified before the House Committee on Small Business that progress has been made but "we know there's more work to do."[142] She testified that "At the front-end, it means more upfront certification and eligibility. For small businesses already in the program, it means more efforts with compliance and site visits. And if they're found to be out of compliance, it means pursuing and removing bad actors."[143] Also, in its FY2012 congressional budget justification, the SBA indicated that

> the Agency will continue to work toward eliminating fraud, waste, abuse and mismanagement in the HUBZone program. Site visits will be integrated into the certification and monitoring processes, which will require considerable coordination with and support from SBA field

> offices. Moreover, more robust portfolio monitoring initiatives will be established. These initiatives include annual program examinations of firms, audits of firms receiving HUBZone contracts, and increased trigger-based reviews prompted by changes within the firm such as change of address or ownership or reports from third party referrals.[144]

One of the immediate by-products of the SBA's new business processes was an increase in the processing time for new HUBZone certifications. In the past, the SBA had a self-imposed goal of making those certifications within 30 calendar days after receipt of a complete application package, subject to the need for additional information or clarification of information contained in the application. Now, depending on the complexity of the application and the need for additional information, the SBA takes 5 to 12 months to make those certifications. It remains to be determined if the SBA's new processes will reduce the incidence of fraud within the program. The resolution of that question could determine the future of the HUBZone program.

End Notes

[1] U.S. Small Business Administration, Fiscal Year 2012 Congressional Budget Justification and FY2010 Annual Performance Report (Washington: GPO, 2011), p. 29.

[2] Henry Beale and Nicola Deas, "The HUBZone Program Report," Washington, DC: Microeconomic Applications, Inc., prepared for the U.S. Small Business Administration, Office of Advocacy, May 2008, p. i, http://www.sba.gov/advo/research/rs325tot.pdf. Sole-source awards under the HUBZone program can be made only if the anticipated award price of the contract will not exceed $6.5 million for manufacturing contracts or $4.0 million for other contract opportunities, and the contracting officer believes that the award can be made at a fair and reasonable price. See 13 C.F.R. § 126.612; 15 U.S.C. § 657a(b)(2)(A)(i)-(iii) (statutory requirements); 48 C.F.R. § 19.1306(a)(1)-(6) (increasing the price thresholds, among other things); and Department of Defense, General Services Administration, and National Aeronautics and Space Administration, "Federal Acquisition Regulation: Inflation Adjustment of Acquisition-Related Thresholds," 75 Federal Register 53129, August 30, 2010.

[3] 41 U.S.C. § 253(b)(1); and 41 U.S.C. § 259(b). For more on competition in federal contracting, see CRS Report R40516, Competition in Federal Contracting: An Overview of the Legal Requirements, by Kate M. Manuel.

[4] Henry Beale and Nicola Deas, "The HUBZone Program Report," Washington, DC: Microeconomic Applications, Inc., prepared for the U.S. Small Business Administration, Office of Advocacy, May 2008, p. i, http://www.sba.gov/ advo/research/rs325tot.pdf.

[5] Ibid.

[6] Federal procurement data generated from the U.S. General Services Administration, Federal Procurement Data System - Next Generation, Washington, DC, https://www.fpds.gov/

fpdsng/. In FY2010, the federal government awarded $3.14 billion through HUBZone set-aside awards, $65.3 million in HUBZone sole source awards, and $376 million in HUBZone price evaluation preference awards.

[7] U.S. Small Business Administration, Fiscal Year 2012 Congressional Budget Justification and FY 2010 Annual Performance Report (Washington: GPO, 2011), p. 24.

[8] U.S. Small Business Administration, Fiscal Year 2012 Congressional Budget Justification and FY 2010 Annual Performance Report (Washington: GPO, 2011), p. 18. Note: Congress provides an appropriation for the SBA's non-credit programs ($185.3 million in FY2011) and includes guidance in its accompanying committee report concerning funding for the HUBZone program. The FY2011 appropriation amount cited here ($2.2 million) is the appropriation amount provided by the SBA in FY2010, which was continued through FY2011 by P.L. 112-8, the Further Additional Continuing Appropriations Amendments, 2011.

[9] U.S. Congress, House Committee on Small Business, Full Committee Hearing on Oversight of the Small Business Administration and Its Programs, 111th Cong., 1st sess., March 25, 2009, Small Business Committee Doc. 111-012 (Washington: GPO, 2009), pp. 1-3, 28-31.

[10] U.S. Small Business Administration, "Small Business HUBZone Program; Government Contracting Programs," 76 Federal Register 43573, July 21, 2011.

[11] Ibid.

[12] The SBA officially established the HUBZone program on March 22, 1999, when it began to accept applications from businesses interested in participating in the program. The SBA certified its first HUBZone business on March 24, 1999. The first HUBZone contract was issued on April 8, 1999. See U.S. Congress, Senate Committee on Small Business, Small Business Reauthorization Act of 2000, report to accompany S. 3121, 106th Cong., 2nd sess., September 27, 2000, S.Rept. 106-422 (Washington: GPO, 2000), p. 20.

[13] U.S. Congress, Senate Committee on Small Business, Small Business Reauthorization Act of 1997, report to accompany S. 1139, 105th Cong., 1st sess., August 19, 1997, S.Rept. 105-62 (Washington: GPO, 1997), p. 25.

[14] Marilyn Marks Rubin, "Can Reorchestration of Historical Themes Reinvent Government? A Case Study of the Empowerment Zones and Enterprise Communities Act of 1993," Public Administration Review, vol. 54, no. 2 (March/April 1994), p. 162. Note: Sir Peter Geoffrey Hall, the Bartlett Professor of Planning and Regeneration at the Bartlett School of Architecture and Planning, University College London, is often credited for developing the concept of empowerment zones.

[15] Ibid.

[16] Stuart M. Butler, Enterprise Zones: Greenlining the Inner Cities (New York: Universe Books, 1981).

[17] Ibid; U.S. Congress, House Committee on Ways and Means, The Enterprise Zone Tax Act of 1982, Message from the President of the United States transmitting proposed legislation entitled, "The Enterprise Zone Tax Act of 1982", 97th Cong., 2nd sess., March 23, 1982, H.Doc. 97-157 (Washington: GPO, 1982), pp. 1-5; and U.S. Congress, House Committee on Banking, Finance, and Urban Affairs, Subcommittee on the City, Urban Revitalization and Industrial Policy, 96th Cong., 2nd sess., September 17, 1980, Serial No. 96-72 (Washington: GPO, 1980), pp. 205-224.

[18] U.S. Congress, House Committee on Banking, Finance, and Urban Affairs, Subcommittee on the City, Urban Revitalization and Industrial Policy, 96th Cong., 2nd sess., September 17, 1980, Serial No. 96-72 (Washington: GPO, 1980), p. 283.

[19] Ibid.

[20] Empowerment Zones and Enterprise Communities Act of 1993," Public Administration Review, vol. 54, no. 2 (March/April 1994), p. 163.

[21] U.S. Congress, House Committee on Small Business, Subcommittee on Tax, Access to Equity Capital and Business Opportunities, Job Creation and the Revitalization of Small Business, 97th Cong., 1st sess., September 15, 1981 (Washington: GPO, 1981), pp. 22, 23.

[22] Herbert Grubel, "Review of Enterprise Zones: Greenlining the Inner Cities, by Stuart M. Butler," Journal of Economic Literature, vol. XX (December 1982), p. 1616.

[23] In 1987, Title VII of P.L. 100-242, the Housing and Community Development Act, authorized the Department of Housing and Community Development (HUD) to coordinate the community development block grant, urban development action grant, and other HUD programs and to provide the waiver or modification of housing and community development rules in up to 100 HUD-designated enterprise zone communities. No enterprise zone designations were subsequently made. See Marilyn Marks Rubin, "Can Reorchestration of Historical Themes Reinvent Government? A Case Study of the Empowerment Zones and Enterprise Communities Act of 1993," Public Administration Review, vol. 54, no. 2 (March/April 1994), p. 162.

[24] Ibid.; and Sarah F. Liebschutz, "Empowerment Zones and Enterprise Communities: Reinventing Federalism for Distressed Communities," Publius: The Journal of Federalism, vol. 25, no. 3 (Summer 1995), p. 127.

[25] Marilyn Marks Rubin, "Can Reorchestration of Historical Themes Reinvent Government? A Case Study of the Empowerment Zones and Enterprise Communities Act of 1993," Public Administration Review, vol. 54, no. 2 (March/April 1994), p. 164. Also see Sarah F. Liebschutz, "Empowerment Zones and Enterprise Communities: Reinventing Federalism for Distressed Communities," Publius: The Journal of Federalism, vol. 25, no. 3 (summer 1995), p. 128; and Edward L. Glaeser and Joshua D. Gottlieb, "The Economics of Place-Making Policies," Brookings Papers on Economic Activity (spring 2008), p. 157.

[26] U.S. Government Accountability Office, Community Development: Federal Revitalization Programs Are Being Implemented, but Data on the Use of Tax Benefits Are Limited, GAO-04-306, March 5, 2004, http://www.gao.gov/new.items/d04306.pdf; U.S. Government Accountability Office, Empowerment Zone and Enterprise Community Program: Improvements Occurred in Communities, but the Effect of the Program Is Unclear, GAO-06-727, September 22, 2006, http://www.gao.gov/new.items/d06727.pdf; and U.S. Government Accountability Office, Revitalization Programs: Empowerment Zones, Enterprise Communities, and Renewal Communities, GAO-10-464R, March 12, 2010, http://www.gao.gov/new.items/d10464r.pdf.

[27] U.S. Congress, Senate Committee on Small Business, Small Business Reauthorization Act of 1997, report to accompany S. 1139, 105th Cong., 1st sess., August 19, 1997, S.Rept. 105-62 (Washington: GPO, 1997), p. 26.

[28] U.S. Congress, Senate Committee on Small Business, S. 208, The HUBZone Act of 1997, 105th Cong., 1st sess., February 27, 1997, S.Hrg. 105-64 (Washington: GPO, 1997), p. 68.

[29] Ibid., p. 36.

[30] U.S. Congress, Senate Committee on Small Business, S. 1574, The HUBZone Act of 1996: Revitalizing Inner Cities and Rural America, 104th Cong., 2nd sess., March 21, 1996, S.Hrg. 104-480 (Washington: GPO, 1996), p. 17; U.S. Congress, Senate Committee on Small Business, S. 208, The HUBZone Act of 1997, 105th Cong., 1st sess., February 27, 1997, S.Hrg. 105-64 (Washington: GPO, 1997), p. 15; and U.S. Congress, Senate Committee on Small Business, S. 208, The HUBZone Act of 1997, 105th Cong., 1st sess., April 10, 1997,

S.Hrg. 105-103 (Washington: GPO, 1997), pp. 20, 23, 26, 27, 33, 35, 77, 147, 149, 153-157.

[31] 13 C.F.R. § 124.101.

[32] For further analysis of the 8(a) program, see CRS Report R40744, The "8(a) Program" for Small Businesses Owned and Controlled by the Socially and Economically Disadvantaged: Legal Requirements and Issues, by John R. Luckey and Kate M. Manuel.

[33] U.S. Congress, Senate Committee on Small Business, S. 208, The HUBZone Act of 1997, 105th Cong., 1st sess., February 27, 1997, S.Hrg. 105-64 (Washington: GPO, 1997), p. 36.

[34] U.S. Government Accountability Office, HUBZone Program: Fraud and Abuse Identified in Four Metropolitan Areas, GAO-09-440, March 25, 2009, p. 5, http://www.gao.gov/new.items/d09440.pdf. Also see U.S. Government Accountability Office, Small Business Administration: Undercover Tests Show HUBZone Program Remains Vulnerable to Fraud and Abuse, GAO-10-759, June 25, 2010, pp. 2, 4, 5, http://www.gao.gov/new.items/d10759.pdf; U.S. Government Accountability Office, HUBZone Program: Fraud and Abuse Identified in Four Metropolitan Areas (congressional testimony), GAO-09-519T, March 25, 2009, pp. 2-9, http://www.gao.gov/new.items/d09519t.pdf; and U.S. Government Accountability Office, Small Business Administration: Status of Efforts to Address Previous Recommendations on the HUBZone Program (congressional testimony), GAO-09-532T, March 25, 2009, pp. 1-3, http://www.gao.gov/new.items/d09532t.pdf.

[35] U.S. Congress, House Committee on Small Business, Full Committee Hearing on Oversight of the Small Business Administration and Its Programs, 111th Cong., 1st sess., March 25, 2009, Small Business Committee Doc. 111-012 (Washington: GPO, 2009), p. 1.

[36] P.L. 105-135, the HUBZone Act of 1997 (Title VI of the Small Business Reauthorization Act of 1997) designated qualified census tracts, qualified counties (originally only in non-metropolitan areas) and qualified Indian Reservation/Indian Country (originally lands within the external boundaries of an Indian reservation) as eligible. P.L. 108-447, the Consolidated Appropriations Act, 2005, provided HUBZone eligibility for five years to bases closed under the Base Realignment and Closure Act (BRAC). P.L. 109-59, the Safe, Accountable, Flexible, Efficient Transportation Equity Act: A Legacy for Users, provided eligibility to difficult development areas outside of the continental United States.

[37] 13 C.F.R. § 126.103 and 26 U.S.C. § 42(d)(5)(C)(i).

[38] Data provided by the U.S. Small Business Administration, Office of Congressional and Legislative Affairs, correspondence with the author, May 20, 2011.

[39] U.S. Census Bureau, "Census Tracts and Block Numbering Areas," Washington, DC, http://www.census.gov/geo/ www/cen_tract.html.

[40] U.S. Small Business Administration, "How often do QCTs HUBZone designations change?" Washington, DC, http://www.sba.gov/content/how-often-do-qcts-hubzone-designations-change.

[41] 13 C.F.R. § 126.103.

[42] Data provided by the U.S. Small Business Administration, Office of Congressional and Legislative Affairs, correspondence with the author, May 20, 2011.

[43] Henry Beale and Nicola Deas, "The HUBZone Program Report," Washington, DC: Microeconomic Applications, Inc., prepared for the U.S. Small Business Administration, Office of Advocacy, May 2008, p. 146, http://www.sba.gov/ advo/research/rs325tot.pdf.

[44] U.S. Small Business Administration, "Small Business HUBZone Program; Government Contracting Programs," 76 Federal Register 43572, July 21, 2011.

[45] U.S. Small Business Administration, "Small Business HUBZone Program; Government Contracting Programs," 76 Federal Register 43573, July 21, 2011.

[46] Henry Beale and Nicola Deas, "The HUBZone Program Report," Washington, DC: Microeconomic Applications, Inc., prepared for the U.S. Small Business Administration, Office of Advocacy, May 2008, p. 146, http://www.sba.gov/ advo/research/rs325tot.pdf. About 13% of qualified non-metropolitan counties were redesignated in 2003 as a metropolitan county due to a change in the criteria for determining metropolitan county status. Those counties were allowed to retain their HUBZone status pending the results of the 2010 decennial census.

[47] Ibid., p. 160.

[48] Data provided by the U.S. Small Business Administration, Office of Congressional and Legislative Affairs, correspondence with the author, May 4, 2010.

[49] Henry Beale and Nicola Deas, "The HUBZone Program Report," Washington, DC: Microeconomic Applications, Inc., prepared for the U.S. Small Business Administration, Office of Advocacy, May 2008, p. 163, http://www.sba.gov/ advo/research/rs325tot.pdf.

[50] Data provided by the U.S. Small Business Administration, Office of Congressional and Legislative Affairs, correspondence with the author, May 20, 2011.

[51] P.L. 109-59, the Safe, Accountable, Flexible, Efficient Transportation Equity Act: A Legacy for Users.

[52] Ibid.

[53] U.S. Department of Housing and Urban Development, "Statutorily Mandated Designation of Difficult Development Areas and Qualified Census Tracts for 2010," 74 Federal Register 51305, October 6, 2009. Note: In making this determination, HUD calculates a ratio for each metropolitan area and non-metropolitan county of the fair market rent (based on the 40th-percentile gross rent paid by recent movers to live in a two-bedroom apartment) to the monthly low-income housing tax credit-based rent limit, which was calculated as three-twelfths of 30% of 120% of the area's very low-income households (which is based on 50% of area's median gross income).

[54] Data provided by the U.S. Small Business Administration, Office of Congressional and Legislative Affairs, correspondence with the author, May 20, 2011.

[55] U.S. Small Business Administration, "Small Business Size Regulations; Government Contracting Programs; HUBZone Program," 67 Federal Register 3828, January 28, 2002.

[56] P.L. 106-554, the HUBZones in Native America Act of 2000 (Title VI, the Consolidated Appropriations Act, 2001).

[57] 13 C.F.R. § 126.103.

[58] U.S. Government Accountability Office, Small Business Administration: Additional Actions are Needed to Certify and Monitor HUBZone Businesses and Assess Program Results, GAO-08-643, June 17, 2008, p. 18, http://www.gao.gov/new.items/d08643.pdf.

[59] Data provided by the U.S. Small Business Administration, Office of Congressional and Legislative Affairs, correspondence with the author, May 5, 2011.

[60] U.S. Small Business Administration, "HUBZones: Latest News and Articles," Washington, DC, http://www.sba.gov/ content/hubzone-latest-news-and-articles.

[61] Ibid.

[62] Data provided by the U.S. Small Business Administration, Office of Congressional and Legislative Affairs, correspondence with the author, May 5, 2011. There were 7,567 certified HUBZone businesses in April 2010.

[63] Employees must live in a primary residence within that area for at least 180 days or be a currently registered voter in that area. The HUBZone definition of employee changed on May 3, 2010. Previously, the definition was based on full-time equivalency and only permanent positions were counted. Effective May 3, 2010, "employee means all individuals

employed on a full-time, part-time, or other basis, so long as that individual works a minimum of 40 hours per month. This includes employees obtained from a temporary employee agency, leasing concern, or through a union agreement or co-employed pursuant to a professional employer organization agreement." See U.S. Small Business Administration, "HUBZone and Government Contracting," 74 Federal Register 56702, November 3, 2009.

[64] 13 C.F.R. § 126.200.

[65] 13 C.F.R. § 126.306.

[66] 13 C.F.R. § 126.401.

[67] Ibid.

[68] U.S. Small Business Administration, Fiscal Year 2011 Congressional Budget Justification and FY2009 Annual Performance Report, Washington, DC, pp. 72, 73, http://www.sba.gov/idc/groups/public/documents/sba_homepage/fy_2011_cbj_09_apr.pdf.

[69] 13 C.F.R. § 126.500.

[70] 13 C.F.R. § 126.501.

[71] P.L. 95-507, a bill to amend the Small Business Act and the Small Business Investment Act of 1958.

[72] P.L. 100-656, the Business Opportunity Development Reform Act of 1988.

[73] Ibid.

[74] Ibid.

[75] P.L. 111-240, the Small Business Jobs Act of 2010, Sec. 1347. Small Business Contracting Parity.

[76] 15 U.S.C. § 644(g)(1)-(2).

[77] U.S. General Services Administration, Federal Procurement Data System - Next Generation, Washington, DC, https://www.fpds.gov/fpdsng/.

[78] U.S. Government Accountability Office, HUBZone Program: Fraud and Abuse Identified in Four Metropolitan Areas, GAO-09-519T, March 25, 2009, p. 2, http://www.gao.gov/new.items/d09519t.pdf.

[79] U.S. Government Accountability Office, Small Business Administration: Additional Actions are Needed to Certify and Monitor HUBZone Businesses and Assess Program Results, GAO-08-643, June 17, 2008, pp. 3-5, 22-30, 33-37, http://www.gao.gov/new.items/d08643.pdf; U.S. Government Accountability Office, Small Business Administration: Status of Efforts to Address Previous Recommendations on the HUBZone Program, GAO-09-532T, March 25, 2009, pp. 3, 8, 9, http://www.gao.gov/new.items/d09532t.pdf; and U.S. Government Accountability Office, Small Business Administration: Undercover Tests Show HUBZone Program Remains Vulnerable to Fraud and Abuse, GAO-10-759, June 25, 2010, http://www.gao.gov/new.items/d10759.pdf.

[80] Henry Beale and Nicola Deas, "The HUBZone Program Report," Washington, DC: Microeconomic Applications, Inc., prepared for the U.S. Small Business Administration, Office of Advocacy, May 2008, p. 136, http://www.sba.gov/ advo/research/rs325tot.pdf.

[81] DGR Assocs., Inc. v. United States, 2010 U.S. Claims LEXIS 588 (August 13, 2010); and Mission Critical Solutions v. United States, 2010 U.S. Claims LEXIS 36 (March 2, 2010).

[82] For further information and legal analysis, see CRS Report R40591, Set-Asides for Small Businesses: Recent Developments in the Law Regarding Precedence Among the Set-Aside Programs and Set-Asides Under Indefinite-Delivery/Indefinite-Quantity Contracts, by Kate M. Manuel. Also see U.S. Government Accountability Office, Mission Critical Solutions, B-401057, May 4, 2009, http://www.gao.gov/decisions/bidpro/401057.pdf; and Office of Legal Counsel, Department of Justice, "Permissibility of Small Business Administration

Regulations Implementing the Historically Underutilized Business Zone, 8(a) Business Development, and Service-Disabled Veteran-Owned Small Business Concern Programs," August 21, 2009, http://www.justice.gov/olc/2009/sba-hubzone-opinion082109.pdf.

[83] For further analysis of the 8(a) program, see CRS Report R40744, The "8(a) Program" for Small Businesses Owned and Controlled by the Socially and Economically Disadvantaged: Legal Requirements and Issues, by John R. Luckey and Kate M. Manuel.

[84] P.L. 108-375, Ronald W. Reagan National Defense Authorization Act for Fiscal Year 2005, Sec. 807. Inflation adjustment of acquisition-related dollar thresholds requires an adjustment for inflation every five years of all acquisition-related thresholds. See Department of Defense, General Services Administration, and National Aeronautics and Space Administration, "Federal Acquisition Regulation: Inflation Adjustment of Acquisition-Related Thresholds," 75 Federal Register 53129, August 30, 2010.

[85] U.S. Small Business Administration, Office of the Inspector General, "Audit Report of the Eligibility of 15 HUBZone Companies and a Review of the HUBZone Empowerment Contracting Program's Internal Controls," Washington, DC, January 22, 2003, http://www.sba.gov/idc/groups/public/documents/sba/oig_gcbd_03-05.pdf.

[86] Ibid., p. 3.

[87] U.S. Small Business Administration, Office of the Inspector General, "HUBZone Program Examination and Recertification Processes," Washington, DC, May 23, 2006, p. 5, http://www.sba.gov/idc/groups/public/documents/sba/ oig_gcbd_6-23.pdf.

[88] U.S. Small Business Administration, "SBA Budget Request & Performance Plan: FY2004 Congressional Submission," Washington, DC, p. 44, http://www.sba.gov/idc/groups/public/documents/sba_homepage/ serv_abt_budget_3.pdf.

[89] U.S. Small Business Administration, Office of the Inspector General, "HUBZone Program Examination and Recertification Processes," Washington, DC, May 23, 2006, pp. 3, 6, http://www.sba.gov/idc/groups/public/documents/ sba/oig_gcbd_6-23.pdf.

[90] U.S. Congress, House Committee on Small Business, Full Committee Hearing to Consider Legislation Updating and Improving the SBA's Contracting Programs, 110th Cong., 1st sess., October 4, 2007, Serial Number 110-50 (Washington: GPO, 2007), p. 6.

[91] U.S. Government Accountability Office, Small Business Administration: Additional Actions are Needed to Certify and Monitor HUBZone Businesses and Assess Program Results, GAO-08-643, June 17, 2008, p. i, http://www.gao.gov/new.items/d08643.pdf.

[92] Ibid., pp. 1-5.

[93] U.S. Government Accountability Office, HUBZone Program: SBA's Control Weaknesses Exposed the Government to Fraud and Abuse, GAO-08-964T, July 17, 2008, pp. i, 4, 5, 7-9, http://www.gao.gov/new.items/d08964t.pdf.

[94] Ibid.

[95] Ibid.

[96] Ibid., pp. 5, 10-20.

[97] U.S. Small Business Administration, Fiscal Year 2010 Congressional Budget Justification, Washington, DC, p. 65, http://www.sba.gov/sites/default/files/Congressional_Budget_Justification_2010.pdf.

[98] U.S. Government Accountability Office, HUBZone Program: Fraud and Abuse Identified in Four Metropolitan Areas, GAO-09-440, March 25, 2009, p. 2, http://www.gao.gov/new.items/d09440.pdf.

[99] U.S. Government Accountability Office, Small Business Administration: Status of Efforts to Address Previous Recommendations on the HUBZone Program, GAO-09-532T, March 25, 2009, pp. 5-8, http://www.gao.gov/new.items/d09532t.pdf.

[100] U.S. Government Accountability Office, HUBZone Program: Fraud and Abuse Identified in Four Metropolitan Areas, GAO-09-440, March 25, 2009, p. 7, http://www.gao.gov/new.items/d09440.pdf.

[101] U.S. Small Business Administration, Fiscal Year 2011 Congressional Budget Justification and FY2009 Annual Performance Report, Washington, DC, pp. 72, 73, http://www.sba.gov/idc/groups/public/documents/sba_homepage/fy_2011_cbj_09_apr.pdf.

[102] Ibid., p. 76.

[103] Ibid., pp. 72, 73.

[104] Testimony of Karen G. Mills, SBA Administrator, before the U.S. House of Representatives Committee on Small Business, "Accountability Update," Washington, DC, April 21, 2010, http://www.house.gov/smbiz/democrats/hearings/hearing-04-21-10-oversight/Mills.pdf.

[105] U.S. Small Business Administration, "Application processing times remain significant, but are now decreasing," Washington, DC, http://www.sbaonline.sba.gov/hubzone/new/index.html.

[106] Data provided by the U.S. Small Business Administration, Office of Congressional and Legislative Affairs, correspondence with the author, May 4, 2010.

[107] U.S. Small Business Administration, "Application processing times remain significant, but are now decreasing," Washington, DC, http://www.sba.gov/hubzone/new/index.html.

[108] U.S. Government Accountability Office, Small Business Administration: Undercover Tests Show HUBZone Program Remains Vulnerable to Fraud and Abuse, GAO-10-759, June 25, 2010, Highlights section and p. 2, http://www.gao.gov/new.items/d10759.pdf.

[109] Ibid., p. 4.

[110] Ibid.

[111] Ibid., Highlights section.

[112] U.S. Government Accountability Office, Small Business Administration: Undercover Tests Show HUBZone Program Remains Vulnerable to Fraud and Abuse, GAO-10-920T, July 28, 2010, p. 3, http://www.gao.gov/new.items/d10920t.pdf.

[113] Ibid.

[114] Ibid.

[115] Ibid.

[116] Ibid.

[117] The bill's sponsor, Senator Olympia Snowe, introduced similar legislation in 2010, S. 3020, the HUBZone Improvement Act of 2010. See Senator Olympia Snowe, "Statements on Introduced Bills and Joint Resolutions," remarks in the Senate, Congressional Record, daily edition, vol. 156 (February 23, 2010), p. S702.

[118] U.S. Congress, House Committee on Small Business, Full Committee Hearing on Oversight of the Small Business Administration and its Programs, 111th Cong., 1st sess., March 25, 2009, Small Business Committee Document Number 111-012 (Washington: GPO, 2009), pp. 4-27, 32-38; Testimony of Karen G. Mills, SBA Administrator, before the U.S. House of Representatives Committee on Small Business, "Accountability Update," Washington, DC, April 21, 2010, http://www.house.gov/smbiz/democrats/hearings/hearing-04-21-10-oversight/Mills.pdf; U.S. Small Business Administration, Fiscal Year 2011 Congressional Budget Justification and FY2009 Annual Performance Report, Washington, DC, pp. 72, 73, http://www.sba.gov/idc/groups/public/documents/sba_homepage/fy_2011_cbj_09_apr.pdf; and U.S. Small Business Administration, Fiscal Year 2012 Congressional Budget Justification and FY2010 Annual Performance Report, Washington, DC, pp. 77-79, http://www.sba.gov/sites/default/files/FINAL%20FY%202012%20CBJ%20FY%202010%20APR_0.pdf.

[119] U.S. Government Accountability Office, Small Business Administration: Additional Actions are Needed to Certify and Monitor HUBZone Businesses and Assess Program Results, GAO-08-643, June 17, 2008, p. 5, http://www.gao.gov/new.items/d08643.pdf.

[120] Ibid., p. 34.

[121] Ibid., p. 45.

[122] Ibid., p. 46.

[123] U.S. Government Accountability Office, Small Business Administration: Status of Efforts to Address Previous Recommendations on the HUBZone Program, GAO-09-532T, March 25, 2009, p. 8, http://www.gao.gov/new.items/d09532t.pdf.

[124] Henry Beale and Nicola Deas, "The HUBZone Program Report," Washington, DC: Microeconomic Applications, Inc., prepared for the U.S. Small Business Administration, Office of Advocacy, May 2008, pp. i–iii, http://www.sba.gov/advo/research/rs325tot.pdf.

[125] U.S. Small Business Administration, "Notice of methodology for measuring the economic impact of the HUBZone Program," 73 Federal Register 46698-46703, August 11, 2008.

[126] Ibid., p. 46701.

[127] U.S. Government Accountability Office, Small Business Administration: Status of Efforts to Address Previous Recommendations on the HUBZone Program, GAO-09-532T, March 25, 2009, p. 9, http://www.gao.gov/new.items/d09532t.pdf.

[128] Ibid.

[129] U.S. Small Business Administration, Fiscal Year 2011 Congressional Budget Justification and FY2009 Annual Performance Report, Washington, DC, p. 73, http://www.sba.gov/idc/groups/public/documents/sba_homepage/fy_2011_cbj_09_apr.pdf.

[130] Ibid.

[131] S. 633, the Small Business Contracting Fraud Prevention Act of 2011, Sec. 6. HUBZone Improvements.

[132] Ibid.

[133] U.S. Congress, House Committee on Small Business, Full Committee Hearing on Oversight of the Small Business Administration and its Programs, 111th Cong., 1st sess., March 25, 2009, Small Business Committee Document Number 111-012 (Washington: GPO, 2009), pp. 4-27, 32-38; U.S. Small Business Administration, Fiscal Year 2011 Congressional Budget Justification and FY2009 Annual Performance Report, Washington, DC, pp. 72, 73, http://www.sba.gov/sites/default/files/Congressional_Budget_Justification.pdf; and U.S. Small Business Administration, Fiscal Year 2012 Congressional Budget Justification and FY2010 Annual Performance Report, Washington, DC, pp. 77-79, http://www.sba.gov/sites/default/files/FINAL%20FY%202012%20CBJ%20FY%202010%20APR.pdf.

[134] U.S. Small Business Administration, Office of Entrepreneurial Development, "Impact Study of Entrepreneurial Development Resources," September 13, 2010, http://www.sba.gov/sites/default/files/09-10%20SBA%20ED%20Resources%20 Impact%20Study%20Final%20Report.pdf.

[135] Ibid., p. 4.

[136] Henry Beale and Nicola Deas, "The HUBZone Program Report," Washington D.C., for the U.S. Small Business Administration, May 2008, p. 159, http://www.sba.gov/advo/research/rs325tot.pdf.

[137] U.S. Bureau of the Census, "About the ACS: What Is the Survey?" Washington, DC, http://www.census.gov/acs/www/SBasics/What/What1.htm. For further analysis see CRS Report R40551, The 2010 Decennial Census: Background and Issues, by Jennifer D. Williams.

[138] CRS Report R40551, The 2010 Decennial Census: Background and Issues, by Jennifer D. Williams.

[139] U.S. Small Business Administration, "How often do QCTs HUBZone designations change?" Washington, DC, http://www.sba.gov/content/how-often-do-qcts-hubzone-designations-change; and U.S. Small Business Administration, "Small Business HUBZone Program; Government Contracting Programs," 76 Federal Register 43573, July 21, 2011.

[140] Henry Beale and Nicola Deas, "The HUBZone Program Report," Washington, DC: Microeconomic Applications, Inc., prepared for the U.S. Small Business Administration, Office of Advocacy, May 2008, p. 136, http://www.sba.gov/ advo/research/rs325tot.pdf.

[141] U.S. Small Business Administration, Fiscal Year 2011 Congressional Budget Justification and FY 2009 Annual Performance Report (Washington: GPO, 2010), p. 72.

[142] Testimony of Karen G. Mills, SBA Administrator, before the U.S. House of Representatives Committee on Small Business, "Accountability Update," Washington, DC, April 21, 2010, http://www.house.gov/smbiz/democrats/hearings/hearing-04-21-10-oversight/ Mills.pdf.

[143] Ibid.

[144] U.S. Small Business Administration, Fiscal Year 2012 Congressional Budget Justification and FY2010 Annual Performance Report, Washington, DC, p. 79, http://www.sba.gov/sites/default/files/FINAL%20FY%202012%20CBJ%20FY%202010%20APR_0.pdf.

In: Small Business Administration HUBZone ... ISBN: 978-1-62100-636-7
Editors: B. Powers and K. Simons

Chapter 2

SMALL BUSINESS ADMINISTRATION: UNDERCOVER TESTS SHOW HUBZONE PROGRAM REMAINS VULNERABLE TO FRAUD AND ABUSE*

United States Government Accountability Office

WHY GAO DID THIS STUDY

The Small Business Administration's (SBA) Historically Underutilized Business Zone (HUBZone) program provides federal contracting assistance to small firms located in economically distressed areas, with the intent of stimulating economic development. In July 2008 and March 2009, GAO reported on substantial vulnerabilities to fraud and abuse in the HUBZone application and monitoring process. GAO also found 10 HUBZone firms in the Washington, D.C., area and 19 firms in four other metropolitan areas in Alabama, California, and Texas that made fraudulent or inaccurate representations to get into or remain in the HUBZone program.

Given the Committee's continued concern over fraud and abuse in the HUBZone program, GAO performed additional proactive testing of SBA's HUBZone certification process, and determined whether SBA has taken any

* This is an edited, reformatted and augmented version of the United States Government Accountability Office publication, Report to the Chairwoman, Committee on Small Business, House of Representatives, GAO-10-759, dated June 2010.

actions against the 29 case study firms GAO identified in its prior work. Using publicly available resources to fabricate documents, GAO proactively tested SBA's application process by applying for HUBZone certification for four bogus businesses with fictitious owners and employees. GAO also interviewed SBA officials and reviewed SBA data about the 29 case study firms. GAO did not attempt to project the extent of fraud and abuse in the program nor systematically assess HUBZone program controls.

WHAT GAO FOUND

The HUBZone program remains vulnerable to fraud and abuse. Using falsified documents and employee information, GAO obtained HUBZone certification for three bogus firms using the addresses of the Alamo in Texas, a public storage facility in Florida, and a city hall in Texas as principal office locations. A simple Internet search by SBA could have revealed these as phony applications. While the agency has required more documentation in its application process since GAO's July 2008 report, GAO's testing shows that SBA does not adequately authenticate self-reported information and, for these cases, did not perform site visits to validate the addresses. Further, the changes have significantly increased the time it takes SBA to process applications. Specifically, SBA took 7 or more months to process each of the bogus applications—at least 6 months longer than for GAO's previous investigations. SBA continually lost documentation for GAO's fourth application, and eventually withdrew it after GAO failed to resubmit the same materials for the fourth time. On its Web site, SBA reported that applicants are experiencing delays during the application process.

SBA has taken some action on most of the 29 firms that GAO previously reported did not meet HUBZone program requirements. The SBA decertified 16 firms from the HUBZone program, and another 8 firms voluntarily withdrew. While GAO maintains all 29 firms did not meet requirements at the time of its review, SBA stated that the other 5 firms were in compliance at the time of its own review and so remain certified. Since GAO's March 2009 report, 17 of the 29 companies have received more than $66 million in federal obligations for new contracts. GAO recently reported that one firm has also defrauded the SBA 8(a) program. Because the SBA did not promptly debar the firm from federal contracts, it was able to fraudulently receive an additional $600,000 in noncompetitive 8(a) federal contracts since GAO's last report. SBA recently proposed debarring this firm.

Source: GAO.

National Historic Landmark Address (The Alamo) Used by GAO as Principal Office Location for a Bogus HUBZone Firm.

ABBREVIATIONS

DOJ	Department of Justice
HUBZone	Historically Underutilized Business Zone
ISDC	Interagency Suspension and Debarment Committee
ORCA	Online Representations and Certifications Application
SBA	Small Business Administration
SDO	SBA's Suspension and Debarment Official

June 25, 2010
The Honorable Nydia M. Velázquez
Chairwoman
Committee on Small Business
House of Representatives

Dear Madam Chairwoman:

In fiscal year 2009, federal agencies obligated nearly $3 billion in sole source or set-aside contracts to firms participating in the Historically Underutilized Business Zone (HUBZone) program, which we have shown to be vulnerable to fraud and abuse.[1] Administered by the Small Business Administration (SBA), this program is meant to spur economic growth in underdeveloped areas by helping qualified small businesses secure federal contracts. Qualified businesses located in HUBZones—economically distressed areas with low income levels or high unemployment rates—are eligible to bid on federal prime contracts and subcontracts available exclusively to program participants, in addition to benefiting from other contracting preferences. The SBA must certify that a small business meets the following criteria to qualify for the program: the firm must be owned and controlled by one or more U.S. citizens; at least 35 percent of full-time (or full-time equivalent) employees live in a HUBZone; and the principal office, where most qualifying employees work, must be in a HUBZone. According to the SBA's Dynamic Small Business Web site, as of March 2010, 9,300 firms were participating in the program.

In July 2008, we testified that the SBA's lack of an effective fraud prevention program meant its application process could not provide reasonable assurance that only eligible firms were being certified to participate in the program. Using fictitious employee and owner information and fabricated documentation, we easily obtained HUBZone certification for four bogus firms. We also identified 10 firms from the Washington, D.C., metro area that participated in the program even though they did not meet eligibility criteria. In March 2009, we reported on 19 additional HUBZone firms from Alabama, California, and Texas that were not eligible for the program.

Because you expressed concerns about continued fraud and abuse in the program, we (1) performed additional proactive testing of the SBA's HUBZone certification process and (2) determined what actions, if any, the SBA has taken against the 29 case study firms we identified in our prior work.

To proactively test the SBA's HUBZone certification process, we created four new bogus firms and applied for HUBZone certification using false information and fabricated documents to meet the SBA's certification requirements. Our applications contained fictitious employee information and bogus principal office addresses. We used publicly available guidance provided by the SBA to create the applications. When necessary, we fabricated documents to support our applications using commercially available hardware, software, and materials. To determine what actions, if any, the SBA has taken against the 29 firms that we found misrepresented their HUBZone status, we made inquiries on our referrals with SBA officials from the HUBZone Program Office, and the SBA's Suspension and Debarment Official (SDO). To identify federal obligations received by the firms subsequent to our referral to SBA, we analyzed data from the Federal Procurement Data System-Next Generation. We also reviewed the SBA's Dynamic Small Business Web site to determine the current HUBZone status of the 29 firms. To identify firms that represented themselves as HUBZone certified, where they may possibly receive benefits from improperly being associated with the program, even after they were decertified by the SBA, we reviewed the Web sites of all 29 firms. We did not review SBA records to confirm actions on the 29 firms or the firms' actions to comply with HUBZone requirements.

Our work was not designed to systematically assess HUBZone program controls or to determine the legal sufficiency of any actions SBA took against the selected firms we referred for investigation. We conducted our investigation from October 2008 through June 2010 in accordance with quality standards for investigations as set forth by the Council of the Inspectors General on Integrity and Efficiency.

BACKGROUND

The HUBZone program was established by the HUBZone Act of 1997 to stimulate economic development by providing federal contracting preferences to small businesses operating in economically distressed communities known as HUBZones. The SBA is responsible for administering the program and certifying applicant firms that meet HUBZone program requirements. To be certified, in general, firms must meet the following criteria: 1) the company must be small by SBA size standards;[2] 2) the company's principal office—where the greatest number of employees perform their work—must be located in a HUBZone; 3) the company must be at least 51 percent owned and controlled by U.S. citizens; and 4) at least 35 percent of the company's full-time (or full-time equivalent) employees must reside in a HUBZone.[3] As of March 2010, approximately 9,300 firms were listed in the SBA's Dynamic Small Business database as participating in the HUBZone program.

A certified HUBZone firm is eligible for a variety of federal contracting benefits, such as sole source contracts and set-aside contracts.[4] Contracting officers may award a sole source contract to a HUBZone firm if, among other hings, the officer does not have a reasonable expectation that two or more qualified HUBZone firms will submit offers and the anticipated award price of the proposed contract, including options, will not exceed $5.5 million for manufacturing contracts or $3.5 million for all other contracts. Once a qualified firm receives a HUBZone contract, the firm is required to spend at least 50 percent of the personnel costs of the contract on its own employees.[5] The company must also represent, as provided in the application, that it will "attempt to maintain" having 35 percent of its employees reside in a HUBZone during the performance of any HUBZone contract it receives.[6]

The SBA must ensure that both applicant and participant firms meet and maintain eligibility criteria at the time of application and, if they are granted certification, throughout their tenure in the program. During the application process, firms attest to the authenticity of the information that they submit to the SBA regarding their eligibility. Subsequent to certification, SBA regulations require firms to immediately notify the agency if any material changes occur that affect their eligibility, such as changes to the number of employees residing in a HUBZone or the location of the firm's principal office.[7] Moreover, certified HUBZone firms competing for government contracts must verify in the government's Online Representations and Certifications Application (ORCA)[8] that there have been "no material changes in ownership and control, principal office, or the percentage of employee's living in a HUBZone since it was certified by the SBA." Firms and individuals who misrepresent their eligibility during the application process or while participating in the program are subject to civil and criminal penalties; decertification from the HUBZone program; or debarment from all federal contracts.[9]

SBA's HUBZone Certification Process Remains Vulnerable to Fraud and Abuse

The SBA continues to struggle with reducing fraud risks in its HUBZone certification process despite reportedly taking steps to bolster its controls. The agency certified three of our four bogus firms based on fraudulent information, including fabricated explanations and supporting documentation. The SBA lost documentation for our fourth application on multiple occasions, forcing us to abandon our application. Our testing revealed that the SBA does not adequately authenticate self-reported information—especially as it pertains to information regarding whether a firm's principal office location meets program requirements. For example, for our successful firms, we used the addresses of the Alamo, a public storage facility in Florida, and a city hall in Texas as our principal office locations—locations that a simple Internet search could have revealed as ineligible for the program. While ensuring that a HUBZone applicant's principal office is legitimately located in a HUBZone is a complicated process, the SBA's failure to verify principal office locations leaves the program vulnerable to firms misrepresenting the locations of their principal offices and thus, benefits of the program not going to areas that are economically disadvantaged. Figure 1 below shows one of the acceptance letters we received.

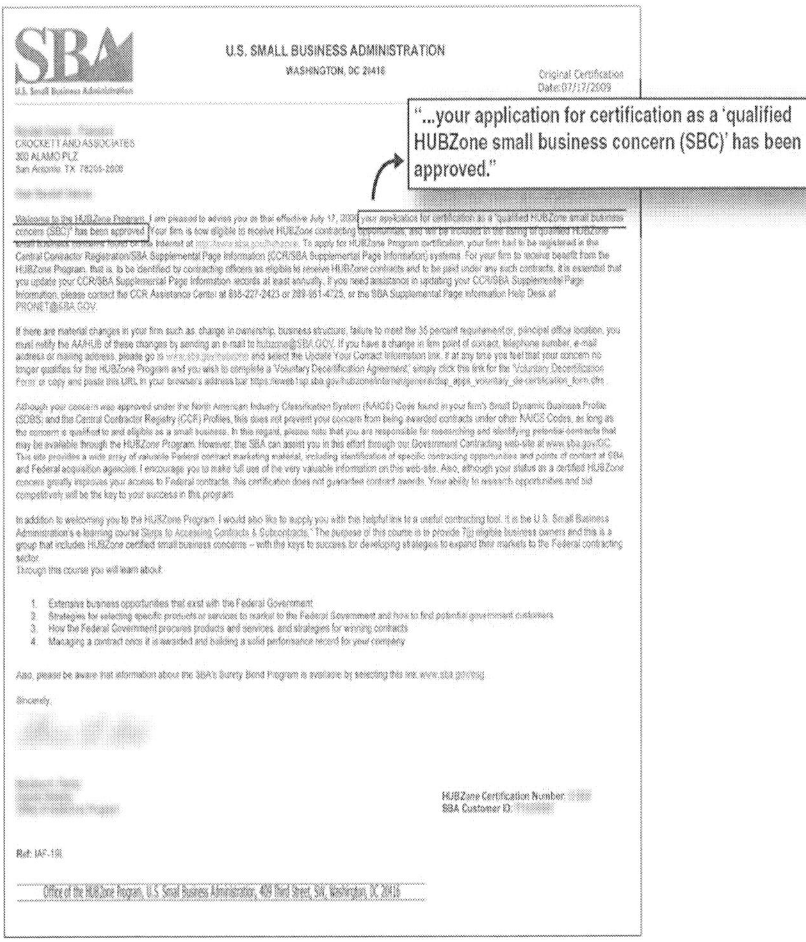

Source: SBA.

Figure 1. HUBZone Certification Letter from SBA for Our Bogus Firm.

In contrast to our last test of the HUBZone certification process, the SBA considerably increased the amount of documentation it requested to support each application and its attempts to contact and communicate with the owners we represented in our applications.[10] However, the SBA also increased the amount of time it takes to certify firms and, by all indications, suspended the use of agency processing time guidelines as indicated by an e-mail that we received from an SBA official and information that the agency posted on its Web site.[11] The SBA took at least 7 months to process each of the three applications from our bogus companies that it certified. In our previous test, the SBA certified our firms in as little as 2 weeks, with minimal requests for documentary evidence. SBA's increased processing times failed to prevent our fraudulent firms from being certified.

As we indicated in our March 2009 report, the SBA initiated a process of reengineering the HUBZone program in response to our findings and recommendations. Though we did not assess the effectiveness of the actions that the SBA undertook to strengthen its internal controls, we were still able to exploit those weaknesses in order to obtain program certification for our bogus firms.

Specific details about each of our fraudulent applications are reported below.

Fictitious Application 1

We received HUBZone certification about 7 months after submitting this application to the SBA. For the principal office location, we used the address of the Alamo, a National Historic Landmark in Texas. We claimed that both the firm's employees were HUBZone residents. Nearly 3 months after submission, we received an email from the SBA requesting a copy of the HUBZone maps that we used to verify the residency of our employees, birth certificates, copies of tax returns for the last 3 years, corporate documents, and a copy of our firm's rental agreement and a recent utility bill. We fabricated these documents using publicly available materials and software and submitted them to the SBA. The SBA then requested a copy of the firm's most recent official payroll records and sought clarification between the number of employees who worked at our firm's principal office and those who worked off site. We were also required to provide additional payroll records and corresponding banking statements with the line-by-line transactions that supported the payments that we claimed to make to our fictitious employees. After all of the requested information was provided, we were approved for HUBZone certification. Figure 2 provides a timeline highlighting the major interactions that occurred with the SBA during the processing of this application.

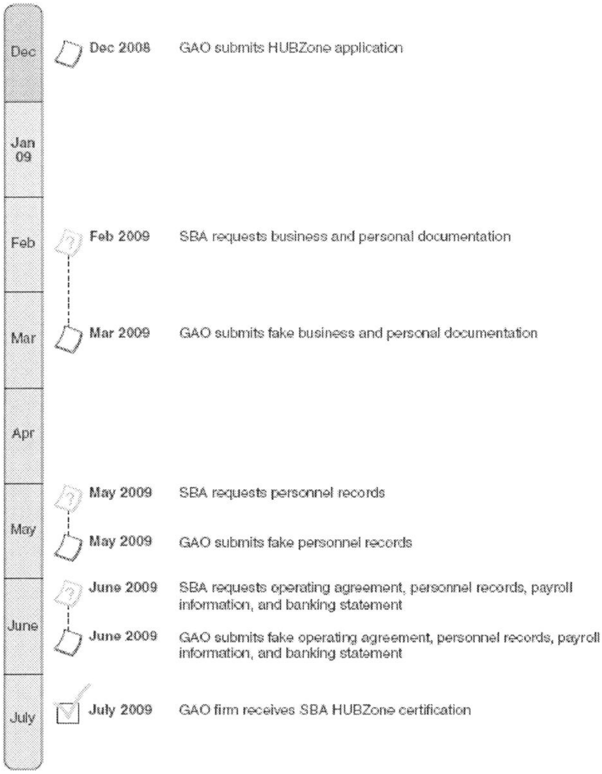

Source: GAO analysis.

Figure 2. Timeline of HUBZone Application.

Fictitious Application 2

The SBA certified this bogus company 14 months after our investigators applied for HUBZone certification. The address we used for our principal office was the same as a rental storage unit in Florida. We claimed the firm was a partnership that employed two individuals who both resided in a HUBZone. To substantiate our firm's principal address, the agency requested that we submit a lease, a recent utility and telephone bill, and a copy of our firm's business registration. To verify the firm's business activity and ownership, the SBA requested copies of our firm's federal business income tax returns for the last 3 years and birth certificates of the two owners, and a copy of our firm's partnership agreement. To verify employee information, the SBA requested copies of each of the HUBZone resident employees' driver's licenses or voter registration cards, a copy of our firm's quarterly unemployment tax filings, and certified copies of the firm's quarterly payroll. SBA also requested tax information and a copy of our firm's most recent payroll documents, which we fabricated and provided to the SBA. Several months thereafter, our bogus firm was granted HUBZone certification.

Fictitious Application 3

After 7 months of processing, SBA approved this bogus firm for HUBZone participation. The address of this firm's principal office was a city hall in Texas. We indicated that two of the firm's employees who worked for the bogus firm lived in a HUBZone. Several months after processing our application, the SBA requested documentary evidence of the firm's location, business activity, ownership, and employee information. After the SBA deemed the fabricated information that we submitted regarding payroll as insufficient to determine our employee information, the agency put our application on hold until we provided further documentation. We then provided SBA with a sworn statement to support information regarding payroll. SBA requested clarification about the frequency that our bogus employees worked from the principal office and granted HUBZone certification soon after.

Fictitious Application 4

After 4 months of processing, the SBA withdrew this application after we abandoned it. We abandoned this application because the SBA claimed that it did not receive supplementary documentation that we repeatedly provided. Two months after the initial submission of this application, we followed up with the SBA to inquire about its status. At the point of inquiry, SBA indicated that our application was being assigned to an analyst for processing. Two months after our inquiry, we received a request for supporting documentation that was similar to those we received in our previous applications. We provided the requested information 3 days after receiving the request. Two weeks later, we followed up to confirm receipt of our documents. The SBA indicated that it did not receive the information that we provided, so we resent the information and requested that the agency confirm receipt. Three weeks later, after failing to receive confirmation on the receipt of our documentation, we inquired about the status of our application. Again, the agency told us that it did not receive the documentation and subsequently gave us one day to resubmit it. If not provided, the agency indicated, our application would be withdrawn. We decided to abandon the application and our application was withdrawn from the program.

SBA HAS TAKEN SOME ACTIONS ON THE 29 HUBZONE FIRMS PREVIOUSLY INVESTIGATED BY GAO

As of March 2010, the SBA has reviewed the status of all 29 firms we referred to it from our prior HUBZone investigations. Since our March 2009 report, these firms have received more than $66 million in federal obligations for new contracts. Not all of these obligations are necessarily improper, and some do not relate to HUBZone contracts. Of the 29 firms, 16 were decertified by the SBA, 8 voluntarily withdrew from the HUBZone program, and 5 were found by the agency to be in compliance with program requirements and remain certified. We did not attempt to verify SBA's work. And although SBA indicated that firms sometimes come in and out of compliance while in the program, we maintain that the firms represented in the cases that the SBA reviewed and determined to meet HUBZone program requirements were out of compliance at the time of our review. In addition, we found that five decertified firms continued to market themselves, through their Web sites, as HUBZone certified even after the SBA removed them from the HUBZone program. Tables 1 and 2 below show the results of the SBA's review of the 29 firms we referred from our July 2008 testimony and March 2009 report.

We also found that one firm continued to benefit from another SBA program even though it misrepresented its eligibility for the HUBZone program and was decertified by the SBA. This firm, a construction firm that was a part of our recent investigation into fraud and abuse in the SBA's 8(a) Business Development Program,[12] also had been 8(a) certified while in the HUBZone program.13 [14] During that investigation, we found that the firm misrepresented its status as a qualified 8(a) firm because it was being controlled by individuals who did not qualify for the program. Because the SBA did not promptly suspend or debar the firm, this firm was able to receive nearly $600,000 in additional noncompetitive 8(a) contracts since our last report. According to SBA officials, SBA has recently proposed debarment for this firm.

Table 1. SBA Actions on 10 Firms GAO Reported as Ineligible for the HUBZone Program in July 2008

GAO case	Primary product or service	Violations found by GAO, December 2007	SBA compliance actions and additional procurement actions through March 2010	HUBZone status, March 2010
1	Information technology (IT), engineering, business management	• Principal office not in HUBZone. • Fewer than 35% of employees live in a HUBZone.	• SBA performed program examination and removed firm from HUBZone program in June 2009. • SBA Suspension and Debarment Official is coordinating with Department of Justice (DOJ) and Interagency Suspension and Debarment Committee (ISDC) to determine whether debarment is appropriate action and, if so, whether SBA should be the lead agency. • Since our March 2009 report, this firm has received $9.4 million in federal obligations for new contracts.	Decertified
2	Construction	• Principal office not in HUBZone. • Fewer than 35% of employees live in a HUBZone.	• SBA performed program examination and removed firm from HUBZone program in July 2009. • SBA SDO determined that debarment was unwarranted based on the evidence of the case. • Since our March 2009 report, this firm has received $9.6 million in federal obligations for new contracts.	Decertified
3	Design and installation of fire alarm systems	• Principal office not in HUBZone. • Fewer than 35% of employees live in a HUBZone.	• SBA performed program examination and removed firm from HUBZone program on November 2008. • SBA SDO determined that debarment was unwarranted based on the evidence of the case. • Since our March 2009 report, this firm has received $3.4 million in federal obligations for new contracts.	Decertified

GAO case	Primary product or service	Violations found by GAO, December 2007	SBA compliance actions and additional procurement actions through March 2010	HUBZone status, March 2010
4	Engineering and construction management	• Principal office not in HUBZone. • Fewer than 35% of employees live in a HUBZone.	• SBA performed program examination and removed firm from HUBZone program on May 2009. • SBA SDO is coordinating with DOJ and ISDC to determine whether debarment is appropriate action and, if so, whether SBA should be the lead agency.	Decertified
5	IT consulting	• Principal office not in HUBZone. • Fewer than 35% of employees live in a HUBZone.	• SBA performed program examination and proposed removal of firm from HUBZone program. • Firm voluntarily withdrew from the HUBZone program in May 2009. • SBA SDO is coordinating with DOJ and ISDC to determine whether debarment is appropriate action and, if so, whether SBA should be the lead agency. • Since our March 2009 report, this firm has received $500,000 in new federal obligations.	Voluntarily withdrew
6	Mechanical engineering	• Principal office not in HUBZone. • Fewer than 35% of employees live in a HUBZone.	• SBA performed program examination and proposed removal from HUBZone program. • Firm voluntarily withdrew from the HUBZone program in March 2009. • SBA SDO determined that debarment was unwarranted based on the evidence of the case. • Since our March 2009 report, this firm has received $630,000 in federal obligations for new contracts.	Voluntarily withdrew

Table 1. (Continued)

GAO case	Primary product or service	Violations found by GAO, December 2007	SBA compliance actions and additional procurement actions through March 2010	HUBZone status, March 2010
7	Acquisition and project management	• Fewer than 35% of employees live in a HUBZone.	• Firm voluntarily withdrew from the HUBZone program in November 2008. • SBA SDO determined that debarment was unwarranted based on the evidence of the case. • Since our March 2009 report, this firm has received $960,000 in federal obligations for new contracts.	Voluntarily withdrew
8	Construction management	• Fewer than 35% of employees live in a HUBZone.	• SBA concluded firm met HUBZone program requirements based on an SBA program examination.[a] • Since our March 2009 report, this firm has received $3.3 million in federal obligations for new contracts.	Certified
9	IT products and services	• Fewer than 35% of employees live in a HUBZone.	• SBA concluded firm met HUBZone program requirements based on an SBA program examination.[a] • Since our March 2009 report, this firm has received $657,000 in federal obligations for new contracts.	Certified
10	IT and logistics management	• Fewer than 35% of employees live in a HUBZone.	• SBA concluded firm met HUBZone program requirements based on an SBA program examination.[a] • Since our March 2009 report, this firm has received $5.8 million in federal obligations for new contracts.	Certified

Source: GAO analysis.

Note: Cases are presented in the same order as reported in GAO-08-964T.

[a]Although SBA indicated that some firms may come in and out of compliance while in the program, we maintain that this firm did not comply with HUBZone requirements at the time of our review.

Table 2. SBA Actions on 19 Firms GAO Reported as Ineligible for the HUBZone Program in March 2009

GAO case	Primary product or service	Violations found by GAO, March 2009	SBA compliance actions and additional procurement actions through March 2010	HUBZone status, March2010
1	Environmental consulting	• Less than 50% of personnel costs for own staff to perform HUBZone contracts.	• SBA did not take any action on firm because SBA concluded that firm met both the 35% residency and principal office requirement. SBA stated that contracting officers are required by the Federal Acquisition Regulations to insert such clauses regarding subcontracting limitations. We believe that SBA should evaluate whether HUBZone firms are meeting the performance-for-work requirements.	Certified
2	Grounds maintenance and furniture	• Principal office not in HUBZone. • Fewer than 35% of employees live in a HUBZone.	• SBA performed program examination and proposed removal from HUBZone program. • Firm voluntarily left HUBZone program in June 2009. • SBA SDO determined that debarment was unwarranted based on the evidence of the case. •Since our March 2009 report, this firm has received $71,000 in federal obligations for new contracts.	Voluntarily withdrew
3	General contractor	• Principal office not in HUBZone.	• SBA performed program examination and proposed removal from HUBZone program. • Firm voluntarily left HUBZone program in June 2009. • SBA SDO determined that debarment was unwarranted based on the evidence of the case.	Voluntarily withdrew

Table 2. (Continued)

GAO case	Primary product or service	Violations found by GAO, March 2009	SBA compliance actions and additional procurement actions through March 2010	HUBZone status, March2010
4	Information technology	• Principal office not in HUBZone. • Fewer than 35% of employees live in a HUBZone.	• SBA performed program examination and proposed removal from HUBZone program. • Firm voluntarily left HUBZone program in July 2009. • SBA SDO determined that debarment was unwarranted based on the evidence of the case. • Since our March 2009 report, this firm has received $2.9 million in federal obligations for new contracts.	Voluntarily withdrew
5	Information technology, general contracting	• Fewer than 35% of employees live in a HUBZone.	• SBA performed program examination and removed the firm from HUBZone program in October 2009. • SBA SDO determined that debarment was not warranted based on the evidence of the case.	Decertified
6	Janitorial	• Principal office not in HUBZone.	• SBA performed program examination and removed the firm from HUBZone program in June 2009. • SBA SDO determined that debarment was unwarranted based on the evidence of the case.	Decertified
7	Medical laboratories	• Principal office not in HUBZone. • Fewer than 35% of employees live in a HUBZone.	• SBA performed program examination and proposed removal from HUBZone program. • Firm voluntarily left HUBZone program in July 2009. • SBA SDO determined that debarment was unwarranted based on the evidence of the case.	Voluntarily withdrew

GAO case	Primary product or service	Violations found by GAO, March 2009	SBA compliance actions and additional procurement actions through March 2010	HUBZone status, March2010
8	Medical services and support	• Principal office not in HUBZone. • Fewer than 35% of employees live in a HUBZone.	• SBA performed program examination and proposed removal from HUBZone program. • In July 2009, SBA SDO proposed debarment for the firm. At that time, the firm was placed on the federal Excluded Parties List System. • In response to the proposed debarment, the firm provided evidence that it was presently responsible and that it was no longer necessary for the firm to be debarred. In October 2009, SBA SDO determined that debarment was unnecessary to protect the government's interests and the firm was removed from the Excluded Parties List System. • SBA SDO did not believe evidence established sufficient grounds for debarment. • The firm voluntarily withdrew from the HUBZone program in July 2009.	Voluntarily withdrew
9	Military logistics and maintenance	• Principal office not in HUBZone. • Fewer than 35% of employees live in a HUBZone.	• SBA performed program examination and removed the firm from HUBZone program in July 2009. • SBA SDO determined that debarment was unwarranted based on the evidence of the case.	Decertified
10	Facility support services	• Fewer than 35% of employees live in a HUBZone.	• SBA performed program examination and removed the firm from HUBZone program in July 2009. • SBA SDO determined that debarment was unwarranted based on the evidence of the case.	Decertified

Table 2. (Continued)

GAO case	Primary product or service	Violations found by GAO, March 2009	SBA compliance actions and additional procurement actions through March 2010	HUBZone status, March2010
11	Construction	• Fewer than 35% of employees live in a HUBZone.	• SBA performed program examination and removed the firm from HUBZone program in July 2009. • SBA SDO determined that debarment was unwarranted based on the evidence of the case.	Decertified
12	Construction	• Fewer than 35% of employees live in a HUBZone.	• SBA performed program examination and removed the firm from HUBZone program in August 2009. • SBA SDO determined that debarment was unwarranted based on the evidence of the case. • Since our March 2009 report, this firm has received $8.9 million in federal obligations for new contracts.	Decertified
13	Engineering	• Fewer than 35% of employees live in a HUBZone.	• SBA performed program examination and removed the firm from HUBZone program in July 2009. • SBA SDO determined that debarment was unwarranted based on the evidence of the case. • Since our March 2009 report, this firm has received $4.7 million in federal obligations for new contracts.	Decertified
14	Engineering and information technology	• Principal office not in HUBZone.	• SBA performed program examination and removed the firm from HUBZone program in February 2009. • SBA SDO determined that debarment was unwarranted based on the evidence of the case.	Decertified

GAO case	Primary product or service	Violations found by GAO, March 2009	SBA compliance actions and additional procurement actions through March 2010	HUBZone status, March2010
15	Facilities support services/construction	• Fewer than 35% of employees live in a HUBZone.	• SBA performed program examination and removed the firm from HUBZone program in August 2009. • SBA SDO determined that debarment was unwarranted based on the evidence of the case. • Since our March 2009 report, this firm has received $9.1 million in federal obligations for new contracts.	Decertified
16	Food service contractors	• Fewer than 35% of employees live in a HUBZone.	• SBA performed program examination and removed the firm from HUBZone program in November 2009. • SBA SDO determined that debarment was unwarranted based on the evidence of the case. • Since our March 2009 report, this firm has received $319,000 in federal obligations for new contracts.	Decertified
17	Information technology	• Fewer than 35% of employees live in a HUBZone.	• SBA concluded firm met HUBZone program requirements based on an SBA program examination.a • Since our March 2009 report, this firm has received $5.4 million in federal obligations for new contracts.	Certified
18	Janitorial	• Fewer than 35% of employees live in a HUBZone.	• SBA performed program examination and removed the firm from HUBZone program in August 2009. • SBA SDO determined that debarment was unwarranted based on the evidence of the case. • Since our March 2009 report, this firm has received $76,000 in federal obligations for new contracts.	Decertified

Table 2. (Continued)

GAO case	Primary product or service	Violations found by GAO, March 2009	SBA compliance actions and additional procurement actions through March 2010	HUBZone status, March2010
19	Temporary help services	• Fewer than 35% of employees live in a HUBZone.	• SBA performed program examination and removed the firm from HUBZone program in August 2009. • In May 2009, SBA SDO proposed debarment for the firm. At that time, the firm was placed on EPLS. • In September 2009, SBA SDO determined that firm did not willfully misrepresent its status to obtain a HUBZone set-aside contract and because of administrative action taken by SBA, that debarment was unnecessary to protect the government's interests. The firm was removed from EPLS at that time.	Decertified

Source: GAO analysis.

Note: Cases are presented in the same order as reported in GAO-09-440.

[a]Although SBA indicated that some firms sometimes come in and out of compliance while in the program, we maintain that this firm did not comply with HUBZone requirements at the time of our review.

CORRECTIVE ACTION BRIEFING

We briefed SBA officials on the results of our investigation on June 17, 2010. Regarding our proactive testing, SBA officials indicated that it was unreasonable to expect them to have identified our fictitious firms due to the bogus documentation that we included in our applications. For example, SBA officials stated that the submission of false affidavits would subject an applicant to prosecution. SBA officials also stated that competitors may identify fraudulent firms and likely protest if those firms were awarded a HUBZone contract. While competitors may identify some ineligible firms that were awarded contracts, it is SBA's responsibility to ensure that only eligible firms participate in the HUBZone program. We suggested that SBA conduct Internet searches on the addresses of applicant firms to help validate principal office locations. We also indicated that if SBA had conducted site visits at the addresses of the firms represented in our applications, those applications would have been identified as fraudulent. SBA officials stated that due to resource constraints, they primarily conduct site visits on certified firms that receive large prime HUBZone contracts.

Regarding our 29 referred firms, SBA officials stated that debarment has recently been proposed for an additional firm. We suggested that if SBA determines that a HUBZone firm is not eligible for the program, it should consider conducting a review of that firm's eligibility if that firm is also certified in other SBA programs. SBA agreed with our suggestion. In addition, SBA provided technical comments which we incorporated into our report.

As arranged with your office, unless you publicly announce its contents earlier, we plan no further distribution of this report until 30 days from the date of this letter. At that time, we will send copies of this report to the Administrator of the Small Business Administration, interested congressional committees and members, and other interested parties. In addition, this report will also be available at no charge on GAO's Web site at http://gao.gov.

If you or your staff have any questions about this report, please contact me at (202) 512-6722 or kutzg@gao.gov. Contact points for our Offices of Congressional Relations and Public Affairs may be found on the last page of this report. Key contributors to this report were Andy O'Connell, Assistant Director; Matthew Valenta, Assistant Director; Lerone Reid, Analyst-In-Charge; Eric Eskew, Agent-In-Charge; Jason Kelly; Barbara Lewis; Jeff McDermott; and Timothy Walker.

Sincerely yours, Gregory D. Kutz; Managing Director;

Forensic Audits and Special Investigations

End Notes

[1] GAO, Small Business Administration: Additional Actions Are Needed to Certify and Monitor HUBZone Businesses and Assess Program Results, GAO-08-975T (Washington, D.C.: July 17, 2008): GAO, Small Business Administration: Additional Actions Are Needed to Certify and Monitor HUBZone Businesses and Assess Program Results, GAO-08-643 (Washington, D.C.: June 17, 2008): GAO, HUBZone Program: SBA's Control Weaknesses Exposed the Government to Fraud and Abuse, GAO-08-964T (Washington, D.C.: July 17, 2008): GAO, HUBZone Program: Fraud and Abuse Identified in Four Metropolitan Areas, GAO-09-440 (Washington, D.C.: Mar. 25, 2009); and GAO, HUBZone Program: Fraud and Abuse Identified in Four Metropolitan Areas, GAO-09-519T (Washington, D.C.: Mar. 25, 2009).

[2] The Small Business Act, as amended, defines a small business generally as one that is "independently owned and operated and that is not dominant in its field of operation."

[3] For service and construction firms, determination of principal office excludes employees who perform the majority of their work at job site locations to fulfill specific contract commitments.

[4] Sole source contracts involve a noncompetitive purchase or procurement process accomplished after soliciting and negotiating with only one source, thus limiting full and open competition. Set-aside contracts reserve an acquisition exclusively for participation by small business concerns.

[5] There are exceptions to the 50 percent requirement, depending on the type of contract; for example, qualified HUBZone firms may meet the 50% labor requirement by using employees of other qualified HUBZone firms. 13 C.F.R. § 126.700.

[6] 15 U.S.C. § 632(p)(5)(A).

[7] 13 C.F.R. §126.501.

[8] ORCA was established as part of the Business Partner Network, an element of the Integrated Acquisition Environment, which is implemented under the auspices of White House Office of Management and Budget, Office of Federal Procurement Policy, and the Chief Acquisition Officers Council. ORCA is "the primary government repository for contractor submitted representations and certifications required for the conduct of business with the government."

[9] If SBA determines at any time that a HUBZone Small Business Concern (SBC) is not qualified, SBA may de-certify the HUBZone SBC, remove the concern from the list, and/or seek imposition of penalties pursuant to §126.900. 13 C.F.R. §126.504.

[10] GAO, HUBZone Program: SBA's Control Weaknesses Exposed the Government to Fraud and Abuse, GAO-08-964T (Washington, D.C.: July 17, 2008).

[11] According to the SBA, the increase in processing time is attributed to its efforts to implement a new, more rigorous certification process it started in late 2008 in response to our findings of fraud and abuse within the HUBZone program. The SBA also stated that this new process, which requires the review of supporting documentation to verify a firm's eligibility for the program, is significantly more labor intensive than the previous electronic-only process that we were able to successfully exploit before. The agency further noted that the HUBZone program is experiencing much heavier application volume than ever before.

[12] GAO, 8(a) Program: Fourteen Ineligible Firms Received $325 Million in Sole-Source and Set-Aside Contracts, GAO-10-425 (Washington, D.C.: March 2010).

[13] The 8(a) program, also administered by the SBA, is one of the federal government's vehicles for developing small businesses that are owned by socially and economically disadvantaged individuals.

[14] This firm is represented as GAO case number 2 in table two above.

In: Small Business Administration HUBZone... ISBN: 978-1-62100-636-7
Editors: B. Powers and K. Simons

Chapter 3

HUBZONE PROGRAM: FRAUD AND ABUSE IDENTIFIED IN FOUR METROPOLITAN AREAS*

United States Government Accountability Office

WHY GAO DID THIS STUDY

The Small Business Administration's (SBA) Historically Underutilized Business Zone (HUBZone) program provides federal contracting assistance to small firms located in economically distressed areas, with the intent of stimulating economic development. In July 2008, GAO identified substantial vulnerabilities in SBA's application and monitoring process that demonstrated the HUBZone program is vulnerable to fraud and abuse. GAO also investigated 10 case studies of HUBZone firms in the Washington, D.C., area that misrepresented their eligibility.

GAO was asked to determine (1) whether additional cases of fraud and abuse exist outside of the Washington, D.C., area; (2) what actions, if any, SBA has taken to establish an effective fraud prevention program for the HUBZone program; and (3) what actions, if any, SBA took against the 10 case study firms in GAO's July 2008 testimony.

---

* This is an edited, reformatted and augmented version of the United States Government Accountability Office publication, Report to the Chairwoman, Committee on Small Business, House of Representatives, GAO-09-440, dated March 2009.

To meet these objectives, GAO identified selected HUBZone firms based on certain criteria, such as magnitude of HUBZone contracts and firm location. GAO also interviewed SBA officials and reviewed SBA data.

What GAO Recommends

GAO makes four recommendations to improve SBA's ability to screen, monitor, and investigate fraud and abuse within the HUBZone program. SBA agreed with three of them.

What GAO Found

GAO found that fraud and abuse in the HUBZone program extends beyond the Washington, D.C., area. GAO identified 19 firms in Texas, Alabama, and California participating in the HUBZone program that clearly do not meet program requirements (i.e., principal office location or percentage of employees in HUBZone and subcontracting limitations). For example, one Alabama firm listed its principal office as "Suite 19," but when GAO investigators performed a site visit they found the office was in fact trailer 19 in a residential trailer park. The individual living in the trailer had no relationship to the HUBZone firm. In fiscal years 2006 and 2007, federal agencies obligated nearly $30 million to these 19 firms for performance as the prime contractor on HUBZone contracts and a total of $187 million on all federal contracts. The map below illustrates the geographical locations for the cases we examined.

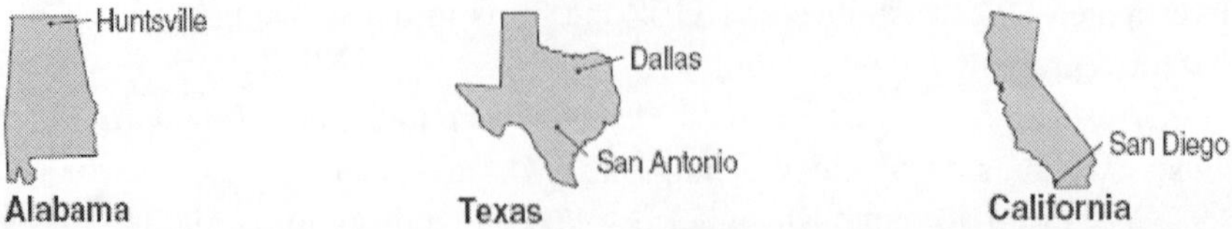

Source: GAO.

GAO Case Study Locations of Fraud and Abuse in the HUBZone Program.

Although SBA has initiated steps in strengthening its internal controls as a result of GAO's 2008 testimonies and report, substantial work remains for incorporating a fraud prevention system that includes effective fraud controls consisting of (1) front-end controls at the application stage, (2) fraud detection and monitoring of firms already in the program, and (3) the aggressive pursuit and prosecution of individuals committing fraud. In addition, SBA did not adequately field test its interim process for processing applications. If it had done so, SBA would have known that it did not have the resources to effectively carry out its review of applications in a timely manner. As a result, SBA had a backlog of about 800 HUBZone applications as of January 2009. At that time, SBA's interim application process was taking about 6 months—well over its 1-month goal set forth in SBA regulations.

SBA has taken some enforcement steps on the 10 firms previously identified by GAO that knowingly did not meet HUBZone program requirements. However, SBA's failure to promptly remove firms from the HUBZone program and examine some of the most egregious cases from GAO's July 2008 testimony has resulted in an additional $7.2 million in HUBZone obligations and about $25 million in HUBZone contracts to these firms. For example, a construction firm from the July 2008 testimony admitted that it did not meet HUBZone requirements and was featured in several national publications by name. It has continually represented itself as HUBZone certified and has received $2 million in HUBZone obligations and a $23 million HUBZone set-aside contract since the July 2008 testimony.

ABBREVIATIONS

CCR	Central Contractor Registration
FAR	Federal Acquisition Regulation
FPDS-NG	Federal Procurement Data System-Next Generation
HUBZone	Historically Underutilized Business Zone
ORCA	Online Representations and Certifications Application
SBA	Small Business Administration
SDO	Suspension and Debarment Official

March 25, 2009

The Honorable Nydia M.Velazquez
Chairwoman
Committee on Small Business House of Representatives

Dear Madam Chairwoman:

Created in 1997, the Historically Underutilized Business Zone (HUBZone) program provides federal contracting assistance to small businesses in economically distressed communities, or HUBZone areas, with the intent of stimulating economic development in those areas. In fiscal year 2007, federal agencies awarded contracts valued at about $8 billion to HUBZone firms. The Small Business Administration (SBA) administers the HUBZone program, one of several contracting assistance programs that the agency oversees. Firms that participate in the program must be located in a HUBZone and employ residents of HUBZones to facilitate the goal of bringing capital and employment opportunities to distressed areas.

On July 17, 2008, we testified before this Committee that SBA's lack of controls over the HUBZone program exposed the government to fraud and abuse[1] and that SBA's mechanisms to certify and monitor HUBZone firms provide limited assurance that only eligible firms participate in the program.[2] In our testimony, we identified 10 firms from the Washington, D.C., metro area that were participating in the HUBZone program even though they clearly did not meet eligibility requirements. Of the 10 firms, 6 did not meet both principal office and employee residency requirements while 4 met the principal office requirements but significantly failed the employee residency requirement. We reported in our July 2008 testimony, that federal agencies had obligated a total of nearly $26 million in HUBZone contract obligations to these 10 firms since 2006. In addition, federal agencies obligated more than $105 million to these 10 firms for performance as the prime contractor on all federal contracts since 2006.

Subsequent to the hearing, you requested that we perform a follow-on investigation. Specifically, you asked us to determine (1) whether cases of fraud and abuse in the program exist outside of the Washington, D.C. metropolitan area; (2) what actions, if any, SBA has taken to establish an effective fraud prevention system for the HUBZone program; and (3) what actions, if any, SBA has taken on the 10 firms that we found misrepresented their HUBZone status in July 2008.

To determine whether cases of fraud and abuse exist for firms located outside of the Washington, D.C. metropolitan area, we first obtained and analyzed a list of HUBZone firms from the SBA's Dynamic Small Business Search database as of September 2008.[3] We then obtained federal procurement data from the Federal Procurement Data System-Next Generation (FPDS-NG) for fiscal years 2006 and 2007.[4] We assessed the reliability of the data and determined that they were sufficiently reliable for the purposes of our investigation. We analyzed the data to identify (1) geographical locations that have both small fragments of HUBZone areas within a metropolitan area, and (2) high concentrations of HUBZone firms that reported obligations on HUBZone prime contracts totaling more than $250,000 during fiscal years 2006 and 2007. Using the above criteria, we selected four geographical areas for analysis: Dallas, Texas; Huntsville, Alabama; San Antonio, Texas; and San Diego, California. Within those four geographical areas, there were 36 firms that met our criteria for further investigation. The firms selected as case studies and the federal obligations associated with those firms did not include subcontracts that they may have received. Such information was not readily available. We conducted site visits for all 36 selected firms and used investigative methods — such as interviewing firm managers, analyzing firm payroll documents, and reviewing information from investigative databases — to gather information about the firms and to determine whether the firms met HUBZone requirements for principal office and 35 percent residency. We also reviewed information about each firm from the Online Representations and Certifications Application (ORCA) Web site.[5] In the course of our investigations, we found instances of HUBZone firms that did not expend at least 50 percent of the personnel costs of a contract on their own personnel. Although our review was not designed to evaluate this requirement, we did report those instances that we discovered in this report.

To determine what actions, if any, SBA has taken to reduce fraud and abuse in the program as well as the actions SBA has taken on the 10 firms that we found misrepresented their HUBZone status, we interviewed SBA officials from the Office of Inspector General, HUBZone Program Office, and the SBA General Counsel. We obtained and reviewed supporting documentation where appropriate. We also reviewed SBA's Dynamic Small Business Web site to determine the current HUBZone status of the 10 firms we identified in our July 2008 testimony.

Our work was not designed to identify all fraud and abuse in the HUBZone program or estimate its full extent for the entire population of HUBZone firms. In addition, our work was not designed to determine whether the selected firms we investigated committed fraud when originally applying for HUBZone status or receiving a HUBZone contract award, but rather if selected HUBZone firms are currently meeting HUBZone requirements. We conducted our investigation from September 2008 through March 2009 in accordance with quality standards for investigations as set forth by the President's Council on Integrity and Efficiency.

BACKGROUND

The HUBZone program was established by the HUBZone Act of 1997 to stimulate economic development through increased employment and capital investment by providing federal contracting preferences to small businesses in economically distressed communities.[6] These areas, which are designated based on certain economic and census data, are known as HUBZones. As of January 2009, there were approximately 9,300 firms listed in the Central Contractor Registration database as participating in the HUBZone program.[7] To ensure HUBZone areas receive the economic benefit from the program, SBA is responsible for determining whether firms meet HUBZone program requirements. To participate in the HUBZone program, small business firms generally must meet certain criteria established by the SBA, most notably: (1) the firm must be at least 51 percent owned and controlled by one or more U.S. citizens; (2) at least 35 percent of its employees must live in a HUBZone; (3) the principal office (i.e., the location where the greatest number of qualifying employees perform their work) must be located in a HUBZone; and (4) the firm must qualify as a small business under the size standard that corresponds with its primary industry classification. In addition, once a firm receives a HUBZone contract, the firm is required to abide by certain subcontracting limitations, which for most firms is to expend at least 50 percent of the personnel costs of a contract on their own employees or employees of other qualified HUBZone small business concerns.[8]

The SBA is legally responsible for ensuring that program participants meet program requirements.[9] If a HUBZone firm does not meet program requirements or fails to notify the SBA of material changes that affect the firm's HUBZone eligibility, the SBA may use a variety of enforcement tools against the firm. Depending on the severity of the infraction, SBA can (1) decertify and remove the firm from the list of qualified HUBZone firms, (2) suspend and/or debar the firm from all federal contracts, and/or (3) refer the firm to the Department of Justice for civil and/or criminal prosecution.

In July 2008, we testified that SBA's lack of controls over the HUBZone program exposed the government to fraud and abuse.[10] Specifically, we identified substantial vulnerabilities in SBA's application and monitoring process by demonstrating the ease of obtaining HUBZone certification.

For example, by using fictitious employee information and fabricated documentation, we easily obtained HUBZone certification for four bogus firms. In addition, we also identified 10 firms from the Washington, D.C., metro area that were participating in the HUBZone program even though they clearly did not meet eligibility requirements.

In June 2008, we reported that the Small Business Administration needed to take additional actions to certify and monitor HUBZone firms as well as to assess the results of the HUBZone program.[11] Specifically, we found that the map SBA used to publicize qualified HUBZone areas was inaccurate. In addition, we found that the mechanisms that SBA used to certify and monitor HUBZone firms did not meet federal internal control standards and provided limited assurance that only eligible firms participated in the program. For example, SBA verified the information reported by firms on their application or during recertification—its process for monitoring firms—in limited instances and did not follow its own policy of recertifying all firms every 3 years. In the report, we made five recommendations designed to improve SBA's administration and oversight of the HUBZone program. We recommended that SBA correct and update its HUBZone map, develop and implement guidance to ensure more routine verification of application data, eliminate its backlog of recertifications, formalize and adhere to a specific time frame for decertifying ineligible firms, and further assess the effectiveness of the program. In responding to a draft of this report, SBA agreed with these recommendations and outlined steps that it plans to take to address them.

Selected Case Studies of Fraud and Abuse Outside the Washington, D.C., Metro Area

HUBZone program fraud and abuse continues to be problematic for the federal government. We identified 19 firms in the states of Texas, Alabama, and California participating in the HUBZone program even though they clearly do not meet program requirements.[12] Although we cannot conclude whether this is a systemic problem based on these cases, as shown in figure 1 below, the issue of misrepresentation clearly extends beyond the Washington, D.C., metropolitan area. In fiscal years 2006 and 2007, federal agencies had obligated a total of nearly $30 million to these firms for performance as the prime contractor on federal HUBZone contracts.[13]

Source: GAO.

Figure 1. Locations of Selected HUBZone Firms That Do Not Meet Program Requirements.

HUBZone regulations also place restrictions on the amount of work that can be subcontracted to non-HUBZone firms. Specifically, HUBZone regulations generally require firms to expend at least 50 percent of the personnel costs of a contract on its own employees. As part of our investigative work, we found examples of service firms that subcontracted a substantial majority of HUBZone contract work to other non-HUBZone firms and thus did not meet this program requirement. When a firm subcontracts the majority of its work to other non-HUBZone firms it is undermining the HUBZone program's stated purpose of stimulating development in the economically distressed areas, as well as evading eligibility requirements for principal office and 35 percent residency requirement.

According to HUBZone regulations, persons or firms are subject to criminal penalties for knowingly making false statements or misrepresentations in connection with the HUBZone program including failure to correct "continuing representations" that are no longer true. During the application process, applicants are not only reminded of the program eligibility requirements, but are required to agree to the statement that anyone failing to correct "continuing representations" shall be subject to fines, imprisonment, and penalties. Further, the Federal Acquisition Regulation (FAR) requires all prospective contractors to update the government's Online Representations and Certifications Application (ORCA), which includes a statement certifying whether the firm is currently a HUBZone firm and that there have been "no material changes in ownership and control, principal office, or HUBZone employee percentage since it was certified by the SBA." Of the 19 firms that did not meet HUBZone eligibility requirements, we found that all of them continued to represent themselves as eligible HUBZone interests to SBA. Because the 19 case examples clearly are not eligible, we consider each firm's continued representation indicative of fraud and/or abuse related to this program.

Table 1 highlights 10 firms that we found to be egregiously out of compliance with HUBZone program requirements. Appendix I provides details on the other 9 cases that we examined. We will be referring all 19 firms to SBA for further investigation and consideration for removal from the program.

The following is a more detailed description of fraud and abuse from 3 of the cases that we investigated.

Case Study 1

Our investigation clearly showed that this firm was being used as a front company because it was subcontracting the majority of its work to other firms. This firm is located in Fort Worth, Texas, and violated HUBZone program requirements because it did not expend at least 50 percent of personnel costs on its own employees or by using the personnel of other HUBZone firms as required by federal regulations. [14] This firm, which consists of 8 employees, has obtained millions of dollars in HUBZone contracts to provide environmental consulting services. At the time of our investigation, company documents showed that the company was subcontracting between 71 and 89 percent of its total contract obligations to other non-HUBZone firms—in some cases, large firms. The principal admitted that her firm was not meeting contract performance requirements required by HUBZone regulations. Further, the principal stated that the firm made bids on HUBZone contracts knowing that the company would have to subcontract work to other firms after the award. The principal added that other large firms use HUBZone firms in this manner, referring to these HUBZone firms as "contract vehicles."

Table 1. HUBZone Firms Making Fraudulent or Inaccurate Representations

Case	Location	Primary product or service	Fiscal Year 2006-2007 Obligations on HUBZone contractsa (reporting agencies)	Case details
1	Fort Worth, TX	Environmental Consulting	$2,310,000 (Department of the Army)	• Firm subcontracted the majority of the work to non-HUBZone firms. Although HUBZone firms are required to expend at least 50 percent of personnel costs performing HUBZone contracts, we determined that this firm has performed between 11 percent and 29 percent of the work on its various contracts to date. • Firm bid on and accepted large HUBZone set-aside contracts even though it did not have the capability to perform them without significant subcontracting. • Owner stated that HUBZone firms are being used as "contract vehicles" for large contracts.
2	Jacksonville, AL	Furniture/ Grounds Maintenance	$920,000 (Department of the Army)	• Firm did not meet principal office requirement. • Site visit to listed principal office found a residential trailer located in a trailer park. No employees were present. Utility and mail forwarding records indicate that no employees worked or lived at the listed principal office for over a year. • Firm did not meet 35 percent residency requirement because none of the employees live in a HUBZone. • Firm president admitted that his firm subcontracted the majority of work to other firms or individuals, violating the requirement to expend at least 50 percent of personnel costs using its own employees. • Firm self-certified that it met the HUBZone requirements in ORCA in February 2008.

Case	Location	Primary product or service	Fiscal Year 2006-2007 Obligations on HUBZone contractsa (reporting agencies)	Case details
3	Arlington, TX	General Contractor	$1,240,000 (Department of Housing and Urban Development)	• Firm did not meet principal office requirement. • Multiple site visits to listed principal office revealed only 1 out of the firm's 33 employees were working at that location. • Company provided documents confirmed that the majority of employees worked at non-HUBZone locations. • Firm met 35 percent residency requirement. • Firm self-certified that it met the HUBZone requirements in ORCA in April 2008.
4	Huntsville, AL	Information Technology	$5,020,000 (Departments of the Army and Navy)	• Firm did not meet principal office requirement. • Site visit to listed principal office revealed no employees were working at the location. • The office where the majority of employees worked was not in a HUBZone. • President of firm admitted that they were not in compliance with the principal office requirement. • Firm did not meet 35 percent residency requirement because payroll records show that only 18 of the firm's 116 employees (16 percent) lived in a HUBZone as of December 2007. • Firm self-certified that it met the HUBZone requirements in ORCA in July 2008.
5	Huntsville, AL	Information Technology/ General Contractor	$2,450,000 (Department of the Army)	• Firm met principal office requirement. • Firm did not meet 35 percent residency requirement because payroll records show that only 8 of the firm's 74 employees (11 percent) lived in a HUBZone as of December 2007. • Firm self-certified that it met the HUBZone requirements in ORCA in July 2008.

Table 1. (Continued)

Case	Location	Primary product or service	Fiscal Year 2006-2007 Obligations on HUBZone contractsa (reporting agencies)	Case details
6	Dallas, TX	Janitorial	$560,000 (Department of the Army and General Services Administration)	• Firm did not meet principal office requirement because multiple site visits to the listed principal office revealed firm no longer occupied this location. • Firm met 35 percent residency requirement. • Firm self-certified that it met the HUBZone requirements in ORCA in April 2008.
7	San Antonio, TX	Medical Laboratories	$250,000 (Department of the Air Force)	• Firm did not meet principal office requirement. • Visit to the company's listed principal office revealed that the location was operated by the principal, but was a study lab operating under a different name. Company website indicates this location is a "satellite" lab. • Company maintains another, larger lab that is not located in a HUBZone. • Firm did not meet 35 percent residency requirement because payroll records show that only 2 of the firm's 7 employees (29 percent) lived in a HUBZone as of December 2007. • Firm self-certified that it met the HUBZone requirements in ORCA in October 2007.
8	Birmingham, AL	Medical Services and Support	$2,220,000 (Department of the Air Force)	• Firm did not meet principal office requirement. • Site visit to listed principal office revealed no employees were working at the location. • The office where the majority of employees worked was not in a HUBZone. • Manager admitted that listed principal office is only used for proposal writing and that the majority of their time is spent in an office which is not located in a HUBZone area.

Case	Location	Primary product or service	Fiscal Year 2006-2007 Obligations on HUBZone contractsa (reporting agencies)	Case details
				• Manager admitted that they only keep listed principal office to meet HUBZone requirements. Firm did not meet 35 percent residency requirement because payroll records show that only 1 of the firm's 11 employees (9 percent) lived in a HUBZone as of December 2007. • Firm self-certified that it met the HUBZone requirements in ORCA in October 2008.
9	Huntsville, AL	Military Logistics and Maintenance	$580,000 (Department of the Army)	• Firm did not meet principal office requirement because the majority of company staff worked in an office that was not located in a HUBZone. Firm did not meet 35 percent residency requirement because payroll records show that only 13 of the firm's 53 employees (25 percent) lived in a HUBZone as of December 2007. • Firm self-certified that it met the HUBZone requirements in ORCA in July 2008.
10	San Antonio, TX	Support Services for Facility	$350,000 (Departments of the Army and Air Force)	• Firm met principal office requirement. Firm did not meet 35 percent residency requirement because the firm's president, who was the only employee, did not live in a HUBZone. President of firm stated that the firm does not have employees to carry out its work but instead uses "leased employees." SBA's regulations state that leased employees do not count as employees for purposes of the HUBZone program.b Firm does not have a current ORCA certification.

[a] Obligation amounts are rounded to the nearest $10,000.

[b] 13 C.F.R. § 126.103.

Source: GAO analysis of FPDS, ORCA, CCR and contractor data.

By subcontracting the majority of its HUBZone work to non-HUBZone firms, this firm is clearly abusing its HUBZone designation and undermining the HUBZone program's stated purpose of stimulating small business development in economically distressed areas. Likewise, because the subcontracting is being conducted by non-HUBZone firms this firm is also evading eligibility requirements for principal office and the 35 percent residency requirement. This firm has been obligated over $2.3 million in HUBZone set-asides during fiscal years 2006 and 2007.

Case Study 2

Our investigation demonstrated that this firm continued to misrepresent itself as HUBZone-eligible while failing to meet HUBZone requirements.[15] This firm, which is a two-person—father and son—ground maintenance services company located in Jacksonville, Alabama, did not meet the principal office requirement, failed the 35 percent residency requirement, and served as a front company—subcontracting most of its HUBZone work to non-HUBZone firms. Our investigation found that the purported principal office was in fact a residential trailer in a trailer park.

As shown in figure 2 below, the "suite number" of the principal office provided to SBA was actually the trailer number.

Source: GAO.

Figure 2. Principal Office for Case Study 2 Firm.

The president of the company claimed that the trailer is the principal office and that an employee lived at that trailer. However, our investigation found that the president knowingly misrepresented and concealed material facts to a GAO investigator. We found that both employees live in non-HUBZone areas that are located about 90 miles from the trailer. Additionally, we verified that the trailer is occupied by someone not associated with the company. Further, our investigation found that neither employee lived in, nor worked at, the residential trailer since August 2007.[16] Specifically, the U.S. Postal Service provided us a copy of the change of address form dated August 2007 that instructed the Postal Service to forward all mail from the trailer to another office in Birmingham, Alabama, which is not located in a HUBZone area. In addition, we obtained utility bill information that indicated that the last utility bill was paid by the firm in August 2007. According to DSBS, SBA most recently certified the firm at this address in April 2008.[17]

During the course of our investigation, this firm provided investigators with questionable documents in an attempt to make the residential trailer appear to be their actual principal office. As figure 3 shows, after our original interview with the president, we found that a new mailbox with the company name had been installed next to other mailboxes in the trailer park to give the perception that the firm resided at this trailer park.

Source: GAO.

Figure 3. Mailbox of Purported Principal Office for Case Study 2 Firm.

Despite the evidence that this firm had not paid utility bills or received mail at this location for over a year, the firm president also provided us with a "rental agreement" stating that their company was renting the trailer until June 2009. The authenticity of this "rental agreement" is highly suspicious given the evidence we gathered and our confirmation that an individual not related to the company was living in the trailer.

For fiscal years 2006 and 2007, this firm received more than $900,000 in HUBZone set-aside obligations.

Case Study 4

We determined that during the period of our investigation this firm represented itself as HUBZone certified while failing to meet both the 35 percent residency and principal office HUBZone eligibility requirements. This firm, which is located in Huntsville, Alabama, and provides information technology services, self-certified in ORCA in July 2008 that it was a HUBZone firm and that there had been "no material changes in ownership and control, principal office, or HUBZone employee percentage since it was certified by the SBA." The firm was certified by the SBA as a HUBZone firm in June 2002.

Based on our review of payroll records and written correspondence that we received from the firm, we determined that the firm failed the 35 percent HUBZone residency requirement. These documents indicated that only 18 of 116 (16 percent) of the firm's employees who were employed in December 2007, lived in HUBZone-designated areas. To have met the 35 percent residency requirement, the firm would have needed at least 41 employees residing in HUBZone-designated areas, thus, the firm did not meet this requirement by 23 employees.

In addition, we investigated the location that the firm purported to the SBA as its "principal office." Our investigation found that no employees were located at this office. Additional investigative work revealed that the firm's primary office was not located in a HUBZone. During the interview, the firm's president acknowledged that he "had recently become aware" that he was not in compliance with HUBZone requirements and was taking "corrective actions." However, the firm continued to represent itself as a HUBZone firm even after the firm's president acknowledged his company did not meet the program requirements.

Based on our analysis of FPDS-NG data, between fiscal years 2006 and 2007 federal agencies obligated over $5.0 million in HUBZone awards to this firm, consisting mainly of 2 HUBZone set-aside contracts by the Department of the Navy.

SBA Has Initiated Steps to Address Internal Control Deficiencies but Has Not Incorporated Effective Fraud Controls

Our June 2008 report and July 2008 testimony clearly showed that SBA did not have effective internal controls related to the HUBZone program. In response to our findings and recommendations, SBA initiated a process of reengineering the HUBZone program. SBA officials stated that this process is intended to make improvements to the program that are necessary for making the program more effective while also minimizing fraud and abuse. To that end, SBA has hired business consultants as well as reached out to GAO in an attempt to identify control weaknesses in the HUBZone program and to strengthen its fraud prevention controls.

Although SBA has initiated steps to address internal control deficiencies we identified in our June 2008 report, SBA has not yet incorporated effective controls for preventing, detecting, and investigating fraud and abuse within the HUBZone program. Internal controls comprise the plans, methods, and procedures used to meet missions, goals, and objectives and also serve as the first line of defense in safeguarding assets and preventing and detecting errors and fraud.[18] Fraud prevention, on the other hand, requires a system of rules, which, in their aggregate, minimize the likelihood of fraud occurring while maximizing the possibility of detecting any fraudulent activity that may transpire. Fraud prevention systems set forth what actions constitute fraudulent conduct and specifically spell out who in the organization handles fraud matters under varying circumstances. The potential of being caught most often persuades likely perpetrators not to commit the fraud. Because of this principle, the existence of a thorough fraud prevention system is essential to fraud prevention and detection.[19]

As of the end of our field work, SBA does not have in place the key elements of an effective fraud prevention system. As shown in figure 4 below, a well-designed fraud prevention system (which can also be used to prevent waste and abuse) should consist of three crucial elements: (1) upfront preventive controls, (2) detection and monitoring, and (3) investigations and prosecutions. For the HUBZone program this would mean (1) front-end controls at the application stage, (2) fraud detection and monitoring of firms already in the program, and (3) the aggressive pursuit and prosecution of individuals committing fraud. In addition, as shown in figure 4, the organization should also use "lessons learned" from its detection and monitoring controls and investigation and prosecutions to design more effective preventive controls.

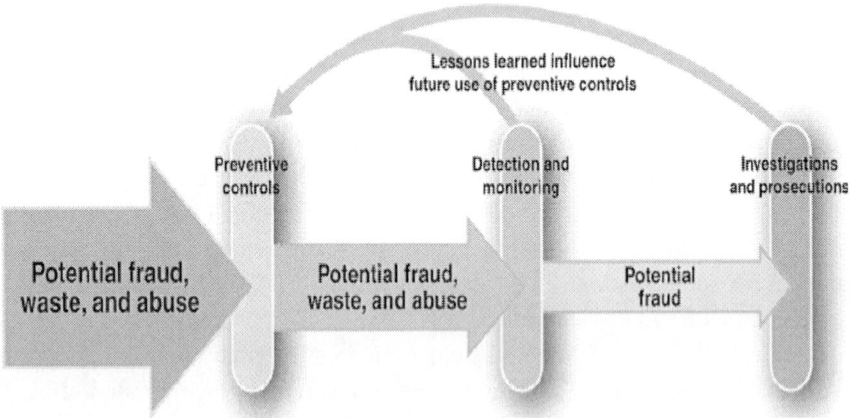

Source: GAO.

Figure 4. Fraud Prevention Model.

We explain the three major fraud prevention elements in this model and how SBA is attempting to address them, in further detail below.

Preventive Controls

We have previously reported that fraud prevention is the most efficient and effective means to minimize fraud, waste, and abuse.[20] Thus, controls that prevent fraudulent firms and individuals from entering the program in the first place are the most important element in an effective fraud prevention program. The most crucial element of effective fraud prevention controls is a focus on substantially diminishing the opportunity for fraudulent access into the system through front-end controls. Preventive controls should be designed to include, at a minimum, a requirement for data validation, system edit controls, and fraud awareness training. Prior to implementing any new preventive controls, agencies must adequately field test the new controls to ensure they are operating as intended.

SBA officials stated that as part of their interim process they are now requesting, from all firms that apply to the HUBZone program, documentation that demonstrates their eligibility. SBA stated that, in the past, it only requested additional information when it encountered obvious “red flags.” Although requiring additional documentation has some value as a deterrent, the most effective preventive controls involve the verification of information, such as verifying a principal office location through an unannounced site visit. If SBA verified purported principal offices by conducting unannounced site visits, such as we did for our investigation, SBA would likely find similar instances of firms attempting to defraud the HUBZone program. In addressing one of our prior recommendations, the SBA issued a Desktop Manual for processing HUBZone applications. [21] The manual provides guidance that alerts SBA staff of circumstances that warrant the need for supporting documentation. Although the Desktop Manual provides discretion to the analyst about the need to conduct a site visit, the Desktop Manual does not provide criteria when such site visits are warranted. In addition, SBA does not screen firms or individuals to ensure that they are not affiliated with prior firms that failed program eligibility reviews. As a result, an owner can change the name of a company that was removed from the HUBZone program to a new business name and be accepted back into the HUBZone program. Further, SBA did not adequately field test its interim process for processing applications. If it had done so, SBA would have known that it did not have the resources to effectively carry out its review of applications in a timely manner. As a result, SBA had a backlog of about 800 HUBZone applications as of January 2009. At that time, SBA officials stated that it would take about 6 months to process each HUBZone application—well over the 1 month goal set forth in SBA regulations.

Detection and Monitoring

Although preventive controls are the most effective way to prevent fraud, continual monitoring is an important component in detecting and deterring fraud. Monitoring and detection within a fraud prevention program involve actions such as data-mining for fraudulent and suspicious applicants and evaluating firms to provide reasonable assurance that they continue to meet program requirements. As demonstrated in our July 2008 testimony, SBA's fraud control vulnerabilities in its application process make detection and monitoring particularly important for the HUBZone program. As a result of SBA's control vulnerabilities, there are likely hundreds and possibly thousands of firms in the HUBZone program that fail to meet program requirements. Although monitoring and detection is an important component of a fraud prevention system, we reported in June 2008 that the mechanisms SBA used to monitor HUBZone firms provided limited assurance that only eligible firms participate in the program.[22] Specifically, we reported that a firm could be in the HUBZone program for years without being examined.[23] In addition, although a HUBZone firm is supposed to be recertified every 3 years, we reported that more than 40 percent of the firms in the program for over 3 years had not been recertified. To address these weaknesses, SBA officials stated that during this fiscal year, they will be conducting program examinations on all HUBZone firms that received contracts in fiscal year 2007 to determine whether they still meet HUBZone requirements. In addition, SBA officials stated that as of September 2008, SBA had eliminated their backlog of recertifications.

Although SBA has initiated several positive steps, SBA will need to make further progress to achieve an effective fraud monitoring program. For example, SBA has not found an effective and efficient way to verify the validity of a stated principal office during its recertification and application processes. In addition, SBA officials stated that although they modified their approach for conducting program examinations of HUBZone firms this fiscal year, they have not established a streamlined and risk-based methodology for selecting firms for program examinations going forward. Further, in order to determine whether firms meet eligibility requirements, SBA needs to incorporate an "element of surprise" into its program examinations such as using random, unannounced site visits to verify a stated principal office. Finally, SBA does not evaluate all HUBZone program requirements during program examinations; specifically, SBA does not review whether HUBZone firms are expending at least 50 percent of the personnel costs of a contract on their own personnel. As a result, as shown by several of our case studies, certain firms are allowed to act as "front" companies, whereby they subcontract the large majority of their work to non-HUBZone firms. This undermines the program's stated purpose of increasing employment opportunities, investment, and economic development in HUBZone areas.

Investigation and Prosecution

The final element of an effective fraud prevention system is the aggressive investigation and prosecution of individuals who commit fraud against the federal government. However, SBA currently does not have an effective process for investigating fraud and abuse within the HUBZone program. Although SBA's Desktop Manual for Processing HUBZone Applications states that an analyst may refer a HUBZone application to the Office of Inspector General or the Office of General Counsel, SBA has not established specific criteria or a process for referring firms that knowingly do not meet program requirements. To date, other than the firms identified by our prior investigation, the SBA program office has never referred any firms for debarment and/or suspension proceedings based on their findings from their program eligibility reviews. By failing to hold firms accountable, SBA has sent a message to the contracting community that there is no punishment or consequences for committing fraud or abusing the intent of the HUBZone program. However, as noted below, the SBA has started the debarment process on 7 of the 10 firms we found to have fraudulently or inaccurately misrepresented its HUBZone status in our earlier work.

SBA Has Initiated Some Enforcement Actions Against 10 HUBZone Firms Previously Investigated by GAO

SBA has taken some enforcement steps on the 10 firms that we found did not meet HUBZone program requirements as of July 2008. According to SBA, as of January 2009, two of the firms have been removed from the program and two others are in the process of being removed.[24] However, SBA's failure to examine some of the most egregious cases we previously identified[25] has resulted in an additional $7.2 million in HUBZone obligations and about $25 million in HUBZone set-aside or price preference contracts to these firms. For example, a construction firm identified in our July 2008 testimony admitted that it did not meet HUBZone requirements and was featured in several national publications by name. It has continually represented itself as HUBZone certified and has received $2 million in HUBZone obligations and a $23 million HUBZone set-aside contract since our testimony. See figure 5 for a reproduction of the continual representation this firm makes on the top banner of its Web site.

Source: Company website.

Figure 5. Reproduction of Web Site Banner for Firm SBA Has Yet to Investigate.

In the written statement for the July 2008 hearing, the Acting Administrator of SBA stated that the SBA would take “immediate steps to require site visits for those HUBZone firms that have received HUBZone contracts and will be instituting suspension and debarment proceedings against firms that have intentionally misrepresented their HUBZone status.” SBA has referred 7 of these firms to its General Counsel for suspension and debarment. However, as of February 2009, according to SBA’s Dynamic Small Business Web site, 7 of the 10 firms that we investigated were still HUBZone certified. Table 2 highlights the 10 firms that we noted at the July 2008 hearing that clearly did not meet the HUBZone program requirements, new HUBZone obligations and contracts these firms received, as well as the actions the SBA has taken against these firms as of January 2009.

As noted in the table above, as of January 2009 SBA has conducted program evaluations on 7 of the 10 firms to determine whether the firms meet the eligibility requirements for the HUBZone program. Based on these evaluations, SBA has removed 2 firms from the HUBZone program and is in the process of providing due process to 2 additional firms to determine whether they should be removed.[26] SBA officials stated that no action will be taken on 3 firms because SBA’s program evaluations concluded that these firms met all the eligibility requirements of the HUBZone program. We attempted to verify SBA’s work, but were not provided with the requested documentation to support their conclusion that the firms moved into compliance after our July 2008 testimony. SBA officials said they have not yet performed program evaluations for 3 of the most egregious firms because they are experiencing technical problems with SBA’s caseload system. As such, these 3 firms remain eligible to receive HUBZone set-aside contracts. SBA is also pursuing suspension and debarment actions for 7 of these firms, and the Department of Justice considering civil actions on 5 of the 10 cases.

Table 2. SBA Actions on 10 HUBZone Firms Previously Investigated by GAO

Previous GAO case[a]	Primary product or service	Case details	SBA compliance actions and additional contract actions through January 2009
1	Information technology (IT), engineering, logistics, technical support services, and business management services	• Multiple GAO site visits to listed principal office revealed that no employees were working at the location and the only business equipment we found was a computer and filing cabinet. • Firm maintained its actual principal office in McLean, Virginia, which is not in a HUBZone, where most of firm's qualifying employees, including the management staff, worked. • According to payroll records, only 21 percent of the firm's employees lived in a HUBZone as of December 2007.	• Firm has received nearly $3 million in HUBZone obligations since our July 2008 testimony. • SBA has not yet performed a program examination. • SBA program officials referred firm to Suspension and Debarment Official (SDO) in January 2009. • SDO submitted a notice of proposal to debar to the company in January 2009.[b]
2	General construction	• GAO site visit to the firm's listed principal office during normal business hours revealed it was one-half of a residential duplex building with no employees present. • Vice president of firm admitted to certifying the firm met HUBZone requirements even though no employees worked at their principal office location.	• Firm received HUBZone preference contract in September 2008 worth $23 million, which includes base and all options. • Firm has received over $2 million in HUBZone obligations since our July 2008 testimony.

Table 2. (Continued)

Previous GAO case[a]	Primary product or service	Case details	SBA compliance actions and additional contract actions through January 2009
		• According to payroll records, only 12 percent of the firm's employees lived in a HUBZone as of December 2007. • Although the firm admitted to failing to meet the HUBZone requirement, as of June 2008 the firm's Web site has a large lettered statement that the firm is HUBZone-certified.	• SBA has not yet performed a program examination • SBA program officials referred firm to • SDO in January 2009. SDO submitted a notice of proposal to debar to the company in January 2009.
3	Design and installation of fire alarm systems	• President admitted that his firm "technically" did not meet HUBZone requirements. • GAO site visit to the firm's listed principal office during normal business hours revealed that it was a virtual office. • Firm operated its actual principal office in McLean, Virginia, not in a HUBZone, where most of firm's qualifying employees, including the management staff, worked. • According to payroll records, only 8 percent of the firm's employees lived in a HUBZone area as of December 2007.	• SBA removed firm from HUBZone program in November 2008 because firm did not respond to SBA's program examination inquiry. • SBA program officials referred firm to SDO in December 2008. • SDO submitted a notice of proposal to debar to the company in January 2009.

Previous GAO case[a]	Primary product or service	Case details	SBA compliance actions and additional contract actions through January 2009
4	Engineering and construction management services	• GAO site visit to the listed principal office during normal business hours found no employees present, the door locked, and mail stuffed under the door. • Firm operated its actual principal office in Beltsville, Maryland, which is not in a HUBZone, an indication that its daily operation is conducted out of this non-HUBZone office. • According to payroll records, only 30 percent of the firm's employees lived in a HUBZone as of December 2007.	• Firm received HUBZone set-aside contract in September 2008 worth $8,500. • SBA has not yet performed a program examination. • SBA program officials referred firm to SDO in January 2009. • SDO submitted a notice of proposal to debar to the company in January 2009.
5	IT consulting	• GAO site visit to the firm's listed principal office found the firm's president and one employee. • According to the president, between 80 to 90 full-time employees worked at a non-HUBZone location in Lanham, Maryland. A GAO site visit confirmed the existence of this location, indicating that the listed principal office does not meet HUBZone requirements. • According to payroll records, only 29 percent of the firm's employees lived in a HUBZone area as of December 2007.	• Firm received about $1.7 million in HUBZone obligations since our July 2008 testimony. • SBA completed program examination in November 2008 and notified firm that it was scheduled for removal from the HUBZone program. • SBA program officials referred firm to • SDO in December 2008. SDO submitted a notice of proposal to debar to the company in January 2009.

Table 2. (Continued)

Previous GAO case[a]	Primary product or service	Case details	SBA compliance actions and additional contract actions through January 2009
6	Mechanical engineering	• Federal agencies obligated more than $27 million on government contracts that were not HUBZone contracts for the firm. • Multiple GAO site visits revealed no employees present at the principal office in Washington, D.C. • Firm operated from an office in Hyattsville, Maryland, not in a HUBZone, where most qualifying employees worked. • President stated that she believed SBA defined "principal office" as "where the principal" (e.g., president) worked. • President also stated that she typically worked at the principal office, but that investigators happened to find her at the non-HUBZone office location. • According to payroll records, only 4 of 78 employees (about 5 percent) lived in a HUBZone as of December 2007.	• SBA completed program examination and notified firm in November 2008 that it was scheduled for removal from the HUBZone program. • SBA program officials referred firm to SDO in January 2009. • SDO submitted a notice of proposal to debar to the company in January 2009. • SBA has still not removed firm from the HUBZone program 3 months after it found the firm was not eligible for the program.

Previous GAO case[a]	Primary product or service	Case details	SBA compliance actions and additional contract actions through January 2009
7	Acquisition and project management	• Firm met principal office requirement. • Payroll documents indicate less than 6 percent of the firm's employees lived in a HUBZone as of December 2007. • Firm self-certified that it met the HUBZone requirements in ORCA in May 2008.	• SBA removed firm from HUBZone program in November 2008 because firm voluntarily withdrew from the program. • SBA program officials referred firm to SDO in December 2008. • SDO submitted a notice of proposal to debar to the company in January 2009.
8	Construction management	• Firm met principal office requirement. • Payroll documents showed only about 17 percent of the firm's employees lived in a HUBZone as of December 2007.	• SBA concluded firm met HUBZone program requirements based on an SBA program examination.c
9	IT products and services	• Firm met principal office requirement. • Payroll documents showed that the firm's only employee did not live in a HUBZone as of December 2007.	• Firm received HUBZone set-aside contract in September 2008 worth $1.8 million. • Firm has received over $20,000 in HUBZone obligations since our July 2008 testimony. • SBA concluded firm met HUBZone program requirements based on an SBA program examination.c

Table 2. (Continued)

Previous GAO case[a]	Primary product or service	Case details	SBA compliance actions and additional contract actions through January 2009
10	IT and logistics management	• Firm met principal office requirement. • Payroll documents show only about 15 percent of the firm's employees lived in a HUBZone as of December 2007.	• Firm has received over $500,000 in HUBZone obligations since our July 2008 testimony. • SBA concluded firm met HUBZone program requirements based on an SBA program examination.c

Source: GAO analysis of SBA information.

Note: See GAO, *HUBZone Program: SBA's Control Weaknesses Exposed the Government to Fraud and Abuse, GAO-08-964T (Washington, D.C.: July 17, 2008).*

[a] Cases are arranged in the same order as in GAO-08-964T.

[b] SBA officials stated that they are giving each company 30 days to reply to the notice of proposal to debar. Within 30 days after receipt of the notice, the contractor may submit information and argument in opposition to the proposed debarment.

[c] We maintain that the three cases SBA examined and determined to meet HUBZone program requirements were out of HUBZone compliance at the time of our review. In January 2009, we asked the SBA for documentation related to its review, but no documentation was provided to us.

CONCLUSIONS

Our work on the HUBZone program to date has shown that numerous ineligible firms have taken advantage of the opportunity to commit fraud against the federal government. The SBA has initiated steps to correct internal control deficiencies, but it still falls short in developing measures to prevent, detect, and prosecute fraud within the HUBZone program. Our work demonstrates that SBA's fraud controls lack important elements needed to screen and monitor firms which has led to HUBZone awards to firms that did not meet program requirements. For example, SBA's failure to verify principal office locations through unannounced site visits has led to firms operating their businesses from locations that are far from economically disadvantaged. In addition, a lack of oversight for monitoring all of the program requirements has allowed HUBZone firms to subcontract large portions of HUBZone work to non-HUBZone firms thereby failing to meet the program requirement that at least 50 percent of the personnel costs of a contract be expended on its own employees. Lastly, SBA's lack of enforcement within the HUBZone program has not had the effect of deterring fraudulent actors from entering or remaining in the program. Going forward, SBA must develop and incorporate effective fraud controls into its overall internal control process that will minimize fraud and abuse in the HUBZone program.

RECOMMENDATIONS FOR EXECUTIVE ACTION

To establish an effective fraud prevention system for the HUBZone program, the Administrator of the Small Business Administration should expeditiously implement the recommendations from our June 2008 report and take the following four actions:

- Consider incorporating a risk-based mechanism for conducting unannounced site visits as part of the screening and monitoring process.
- Consider incorporating policies and procedures into SBA's program examinations for evaluating if a HUBZone firm is expending at least 50 percent of the personnel costs of a contract using its own employees.

- Ensure appropriate policies and procedures are in place for the prompt reporting and referral of fraud and abuse to SBA's Office of Inspector General as well as SBA's Suspension and Debarment Official.
- Take appropriate enforcement actions on the 19 HUBZone firms we found to violate HUBZone program requirements to include, where applicable, immediate removal or decertification from the program, and coordination with SBA's Office of Inspector General as well as SBA's Suspension and Debarment Official.

AGENCY COMMENTS AND OUR EVALUATION

We received written comments on a draft of this report from SBA's Deputy Associate Administrator of the Office of Business Development and Government Contracting. In the response, SBA agreed with three of our four recommendations. SBA stated that it is in the process of re-engineering the entire HUBZone certification and eligibility process, and SBA believes that our recommendations are useful in making necessary program changes to minimize program risk and ensure that only eligible firms received HUBZone program benefits. SBA's written comments are provided in appendix II.

SBA disagreed with our recommendation to consider incorporating policies and procedures into SBA's program examinations for evaluating if a HUBZone firm is complying with the performance-of-work requirements by expending at least 50 percent of the personnel costs of a contract using its own employees. SBA stated that although this requirement is included in SBA HUBZone regulations, it is not a criterion for HUBZone program eligibility but rather a mandatory contract term. SBA stated that contracting officers are required by the Federal Acquisition Regulations to insert such clauses regarding subcontracting limitations. If firms submit bids that indicate that they will not meet this requirement or fail to meet this requirement during performance of the contract, the contracting officer has the authority to reject a firm's bid or terminate the contract for default. SBA stated that it will continue to work with contracting officers to ensure that this requirement is monitored.

While we recognize that contracting officers have a responsibility for monitoring the subcontracting limitation, SBA also has this responsibility. In order to receive HUBZone certification, a firm must certify to SBA that it will abide by this performance requirement, and SBA is required by statute

Case	Location	Primary product or service	Fiscal Year 2006-2007 Obligations on HUBZone contracts[a] (reporting agencies)	Case details
14	San Diego, CA	Engineering and Information Technology	$960,000 (Department of the Navy)	• Firm did not meet principal office requirement because the firm's principal office was not located in HUBZone area.[b] • Firm met 35 percent residency requirement. • Firm self-certified that it met the HUBZone requirements in ORCA in September 2008.
15	San Antonio, TX	Facilities Support Services/Construction	$1,840,000 (multiple agencies)	• Firm met principal office requirement. • Firm did not meet 35 percent residency requirement because payroll records show that only 8 of the firm's 76 employees (11 percent) lived in a HUBZone as of December 2007. • Firm self-certified that it met the HUBZone requirements in ORCA in May 2008.
16	San Antonio, TX	Food Service Contractors	$830,000 (Department of the Navy)	• Firm met principal office requirement. • Firm did not meet 35 percent residency requirement because payroll records show that only 62 of the firm's 239 employees (26 percent) lived in a HUBZone as of December 2007. • Firm does not have a current ORCA certification.

Table 3. (Continued)

Case	Location	Primary product or service	Fiscal Year 2006-2007 Obligations on HUBZone contracts[a] (reporting agencies)	Case details
17	San Diego, CA	Information Technology	$2,090,000 (multiple agencies)	• Firm met principal office requirement. • Firm did not meet 35 percent residency requirement because payroll records show that only 10 of the firm's 43 employees (23 percent) lived in a HUBZone as of December 2007. • Firm self-certified that it met the HUBZone requirements in ORCA in July 2008.
18	Waco, TX	Janitorial	$440,000 (Department of Veterans Affairs)	• Firm met principal office requirement. • Firm did not meet 35 percent residency requirement because payroll records show that only 4 of the firm's 16 employees (25 percent) lived in a HUBZone as of December 2007. • Firm self-certified that it met the HUBZone requirements in ORCA in November 2008.

Case	Location	Primary product or service	Fiscal Year 2006-2007 Obligations on HUBZone contracts[a] (reporting agencies)	Case details
19	San Antonio, TX	Temporary Help Services	$350,000 (Departments of the Navy and Army)	• Firm met principal office requirement. • Firm did not meet 35 percent residency requirement because payroll records show that this firm's only employee did not live in a HUBZone as of December 2007.[c] • Firm self-certified that it met the HUBZone requirements in ORCA in July 2008.

Source: GAO analysis of FPDS, ORCA, CCR and contractor data.

[a] Net obligation amounts are rounded to the nearest $10,000.

[b] We checked this firm's principal office address using both the current HUBZone map located on SBA's Web site as well as a HUBZone map as it would have appeared in December 2007 and in both instances the firm's principal office was not located in a HUBZone area.

[c] Earlier in 2007, a total of 16 people were employed by this company, however at no time did any of the employees live in a HUBZone.

APPENDIX II: COMMENTS FROM THE SMALL BUSINESS ADMINISTRATION

U.S. SMALL BUSINESS ADMINISTRATION
WASHINGTON, D.C. 20416

March 13, 2009

Greg Kutz, Managing Director
Forensic Audits and Special Investigations
U. S. Government Accountability Office
Washington, DC 20548

Dear Mr. Kutz,

Thank you for allowing the U.S. Small Business Administration (SBA) the opportunity to comment on your Draft Government Accountability Office (GAO) Report Number: GAO 09-440, entitled, "HUBZone Program: Fraud and Abuse Identified in Four Metropolitan Areas."

SBA has reviewed GAO's four recommendations for executive action and is submitting the following responses:

Recommendation #1
Consider incorporating a risk-based mechanism for conducting unannounced site visits as part of the screening and monitoring process.

Response: SBA agrees with the recommendation. SBA will develop risk-based procedures for conducting site visits to ensure HUBZone program eligibility.

Recommendation #2
Consider incorporating policies and procedures into SBA's program examinations for evaluating if a HUBZone firm is expending at least 50 percent of the personnel costs of a contract using its own employees.

Response: SBA disagrees with the recommendation to revise program examination polices and procedures for evaluating if a HUBZone firm is expending at least 50 percent of the personnel cost of a contract using its own employees. Although the 50 percent requirement is included SBA HUBZone regulations, it is not a criteria for HUBZone program eligibility but rather a mandatory contract term. When awarding HUBZone set-aside contracts, HUBZone sole source contracts, or contracts with a HUBZone price evaluation preference, contracting officers are required by the Federal Acquisition Regulations to insert such clauses. If firms submit bids that indicate that they will not meet this requirement or fail to meet this requirement during performance of the contract, the contracting officer has the authority to reject a firm's bid or terminate the contract for default. SBA will continue to work with contracting officers to ensure that this requirement is monitored.

Page 2

Recommendation #3
Ensure appropriate policies and procedures are in place for the prompt reporting and referral of fraud and abuse to SBA's Office of Inspector General as well as SBA's Suspension and Debarment Official.

Response: SBA agrees with the recommendation. SBA is developing policies and standard operating procedures for prompt reporting and referral of cases of fraud and abuse to SBA's Office of Inspector General and Suspension and Debarment Official.

Recommendation #4
Take appropriate enforcement actions on the 19 HUBZone firms we found to violate HUBZone program requirements to include, where applicable, immediate removal or decertification from the program, and coordination with SBA's Office of Inspector General as well as SBA's Suspension and Debarment Official.

Response: SBA agrees with the recommendation. Once GAO provides the names of the 19 firms, the HUBZone office will confirm their ineligibility and if appropriate initiate decertification action and make referral to SBA's Office of Inspector General and SBA's Suspension and Debarment Official for action.

As indicated in the draft report, SBA is in the process of re-engineering the entire HUBZone certification and eligibility process, and we believe that the GAO's recommendations are useful in making necessary program changes to minimize program risk and ensure that only eligible firms received HUBZone program benefits. Again, thank you for the opportunity to comment. If you have any questions or require additional information, please contact Ms. Tiffani Cooper, GAO Liaison at (202) 205-6700.

Sincerely,

Calvin Jenkins
Deputy Associate Administrator
Office of Business Development and Government Contracting

APPENDIX III: STAFF ACKNOWLEDGMENTS

Erika Axelson, Gary Bianchi,

Donald Brown, Bruce Causseaux, Eric Eskew, Dennis Fauber, Craig Fischer, Robert Graves, Betsy Isom, Jason Kelly, Julia Kennon, Barbara Lewis, Olivia Lopez, Jeff McDermott, Andrew McIntosh, John Mingus, Andy O'Connell, Mary Osorno, Chris Rodgers, and Matt Valenta also provided assistance on this report.

End Notes

[1] GAO, HUBZone Program: SBA's Control Weaknesses Exposed the Government to Fraud and Abuse, GAO-08-964T (Washington, D.C.: July 17, 2008).

[2] GAO, Small Business Administration: Additional Actions Are Needed to Certify and Monitor HUBZone Businesses and Assess Program Results, GAO-08-975T (Washington, D.C.: July 17, 2008).

[3] The Dynamic Small Business Search is part of the Central Contractor Registration (CCR) database. If a firm indicates it is a small business in CCR, its business information will be populated in SBA's database and can be accessed through the Dynamic Small Business Search.

[4] The FPDS-NG is the central repository for capturing information on federal procurement actions. Dollar amounts reported by federal agencies to FPDS-NG represent the net amount of funds obligated or deobligated as a result of procurement actions. Because we did not obtain disbursement data, we were unable to identify the actual amounts received by firms.

[5] ORCA was established as part of the Business Partner Network, an element of the Integrated Acquisition Environment, which is implemented under the auspices of White House Office of Management and Budget, Office of Federal Procurement Policy, and the Chief Acquisition Officers Council. ORCA is "the primary Government repository for contractor submitted representations and certifications required for the conduct of business with the Government."

[6] HUBZone Act of 1997, Pub. L. No. 105-135, Title VI, § 602(a), 111 Stat. 2592, 2627 (1997).

[7] We previously reported that, as of February 2008, SBA had about 13,000 firms in the HUBZone program. SBA officials stated that they did not maintain data on the reason why there was a 3,700 decrease in the number of firms in the HUBZone program. According to SBA officials, a possible cause for this decrease was that SBA eliminated a backlog of its HUBZone recertifications. SBA officials said that many of these firms were removed from the HUBZone program because the firms either voluntarily withdrew or did not respond to SBA's recertification inquiry after giving them due process.

[8] There are different means of fulfilling this requirement, depending on the type of contract. 13 C.F.R. § 126.700.

[9] 15 U.S.C. § 657a.

[10] GAO, HUBZone Program: SBA's Control Weaknesses Exposed the Government to Fraud and Abuse, GAO-08-964T (Washington, D.C.: July 17, 2008).

[11] GAO, Small Business Administration: Additional Actions Are Needed to Certify and Monitor HUBZone Businesses and Assess Program Results, GAO-08-643 (Washington, D.C.: June, 2008).

[12] These firms had principal offices in or near 4 metropolitan areas: Dallas, Texas; Huntsville, Alabama; San Antonio, Texas; and San Diego, California.

[13] These 19 firms received a total of $187 million in federal obligations in fiscal years 2006 and 2007.

[14] See 13 C.F.R. § 126.700.

[15] This firm attested in ORCA in February 2008 that it made "no material changes in ownership and control, principal office, or HUBZone employee percentage since it was certified by SBA."

[16] We were unable to verify if this trailer was ever used as the firm's principal office.

[17] HUBZone companies must re-certify with SBA every 3 years.

[18] GAO/AIMD-00-21.3.1 Standards for Internal Control in the Federal Government.

[19] Association of Certified Fraud Examiners, Fraud Examiners Manual, U.S. Edition (2007).

[20] GAO, Hurricanes Katrina and Rita Disaster Relief: Prevention is the Key to Minimizing Fraud, Waste and Abuse in Recovery Efforts, GAO-07-418T (Washington, D.C.: Jan. 29, 2007); and Individual Disaster Assistance Programs: Framework for Fraud Prevention, Detection, and Prosecution, GAO-06-954T (Washington, D.C.: July 12, 2006).

[21] We did not test the extent to which SBA personnel are following the instruction in the Desktop Manual.

[22] GAO, Small Business Administration: Additional Actions Are Needed to Certify and Monitor HUBZone Businesses and Assess Program Results, GAO-08-643 (Washington, D.C.: June, 2008).

[23] Since fiscal year 2004, SBA's policy was to conduct program examinations on 5 percent of firms each year. According to SBA, a program examination involves a review of the following criteria: 1) 51 percent ownership by a U.S. citizen; 2) qualification as a small business under the size standard corresponding to primary industry classification; 3) the firm's principal office must be located in a HUBZone; and 4) at least 35 percent of the firm's employees must reside in a HUBZone.

[24] As of February 2009, 7 of the 10 firms were still HUBZone certified according to SBA's Dynamic Small Business Search. One of the two firms in the process of being removed was no longer listed as HUBZone certified.

[25] GAO, HUBZone Program: SBA's Control Weaknesses Exposed the Government to Fraud and Abuse, GAO-08-964T (Washington, D.C.: July 17, 2008).

[26] A firm that SBA has decertified may seek certification no sooner than one year from the date of decertification. If the firm was decertified for failure to notify SBA of a material change affecting its eligibility, it must include with its application for certification a full explanation of why it failed to notify SBA of the material change.

INDEX

D

E

F

G

H

I

J

L

M

N

O

P

Q

R

S

T

U

W